# From
# Indian Corn
## to
# Outer Space

# Women Invent in America

BY ELLEN H. SHOWELL AND FRED M.B. AMRAM

## Acknowledgments

We wish to thank our first line of support — our spouses,
Sandra and John, who gave us the freedom and encouragement to dare to
write this book. We gratefully acknowledge the teachers who provided advice and
inspiration, especially Tracy Lee, Doris Broughton, Judy Grumbacher, and Sara
Anderson. We also thank Sara Anderson for creating the crossword puzzles. The support of
our friends in the Children's Book Guild of Washington, D.C., was enormously helpful.
Jennifer Gabrys and Jacqueline Reid did much of the library sleuthing.

We dedicate this book to all the children who will grow up to become the
inventors who will save our world. Most of all, we send this book, with love, to
our grandchildren — Ariana, Zoe, Stephanie, Douglas, and David —
with wishes for a creative ever after.

. . . . . . . . . . . . . . . . . . . . . . . . .

Copy-edited by Barbara Jatkola
Design and page layout by C. Porter Designs, Fitzwilliam, New Hampshire
Cover illustration by Gary Krejca
Interior illustrations by Brad Walker
Printing and binding by D.B. Hess Company

Manufactured in the United States of America
ISBN 0-942389-10-7

The procedure for "Make Yogurt" on page 77 is adapted from the article "Let's Make Yogurt" by Peggy Ma, which appeared in the May 1994 issue of *Science Scope* magazine, and from *The Joy of Cooking* by Irma S. Rombauer and Marion R. Becker (New York: Macmillan, 1978), p. 533.

### Picture Credits

Courtesy U.S. Patent and Trademark Office: 4; courtesy Ellen Showell: 8, 9; reprinted from *What People Wore* by Douglas Gorsline: 10, 12; courtesy Robinson-Spangler Carolina Room at the Public Library of Charlotte Mecklenburg County: 15; courtesy Fred M.B. Amram: 23, 24, 25 (both), 26, 30; Graphic Arts Collection, National Museum of American History, Smithsonian Institution: 28; Madam Walker Collection of A'Lelia Bundles: 32, 33; courtesy *Chicago Defender:* 35 (both); courtesy Whittier Historical Society: 36; National Archives: 38; photo by Michael Flynn, courtesy U.S. Navy: 48, 50; courtesy Erna Hoover: 52; courtesy Ruth Benerito: 55; courtesy Research Corporation: 56; courtesy DuPont Company: 58, 59; courtesy 3M Company: 61, 62; courtesy Gertrude B. Elion, D.Sc.: 65; courtesy

North Carolina State University Visual Communication: 67; courtesy NASA: 78, 81, 84; courtesy Eve Wooldridge: 86; photo by E. Donald Weiner, Malden, MA, courtesy NASA: 88; courtesy Karen Castell: 91; courtesy Hatice Cullingford: 93; courtesy Myrna Hoffman: 102 (both); photos by Bill Stover, St. Louis, MO, courtesy Betty Rozier: 106, 109; courtesy Ann Moore: 113; photo by Nancy Campbell, courtesy Gabriele Knecht: 114; photo by Irving Solero, courtesy Gabriele Knecht: 116; photo by Bruce Schoenberger, courtesy Carol Wior Inc.: 118; Frances Gabe: 121; copyright Lois Holman from *Rose O'Neill Kewpies and Other Works*: 136; courtesy Michael Nesmith: 139 (both); courtesy Academy of Applied Science: 149.

# CONTENTS

## *About the Authors*

**Ellen Pennington Harvey Showell** has been writing for children since 1971. Her works include novels, plays performed in schools, screenplays, poems, and beginning reader and picture books. She graduated from Berea College in Berea, Kentucky. After some adventurous traveling, she settled in the Washington, D.C., area and wrote for advertising and public relations firms and for the government's VISTA and Peace Corps programs. Her articles have appeared in several national magazines and professional journals.

**Fred M.B. Amram,** an award-winning professor of speech communication and creativity, is currently director of academic affairs at the General College, University of Minnesota. He has written books and articles relating to creativity, women inventors, robotics, and communication. Professor Amram has been curator of several exhibitions displaying the achievements of women inventors. His employment experience in industry and education has led to consulting activities around the world.

# A Message From the Assistant Secretary of Commerce and Commissioner of Patents and Trademarks

ASK A YOUNG GIRL WHAT AN inventor looks like, and the result may be surprising. Gone are the days when a typical description of an inventor would have been "a man with frizzy hair wearing thick glasses and a white lab coat." As more and more women are taking advantage of broader educational and career opportunities, the stereotypical image of an inventor is slowly changing, and the description of an inventor is more likely to be "just like me."

This is such an exciting time to lead the U.S. Patent and Trademark Office, where we see this change firsthand, where every day we are dazzled by improved technologies, and where we hope and pray that the next patent application to pass through our doors will be for a cure for cancer or AIDS.

The economic success of the United States is rooted in the creative genius of our citizens, in the imagination of men and women who turn ideas into products that produce industries that generate jobs that guarantee wages to millions of Americans. I'm sure you know the names of our most famous inventors — men like Samuel Morse, Alexander Graham Bell, George Westinghouse, and Henry Ford — and the industries their inventions started. However, there are other names — hundreds of thousands of names — of inventors we don't know, especially women inventors.

These women deserve our recognition because they also put their stamp on America and added, as Abraham Lincoln said, "the fuel of interest to the fire of genius." I'm talking about people like Sarah Goode, who twenty years after the Civil War became the first African American woman to receive a patent.

In 1993, half the patents awarded to women were in the high-technology fields. And according to the National Science Board, the number of women pursuing engineering and science degrees is steadily increasing. This would no doubt please Florence Parpart, Mary Anderson, and Margaret Knight, inventors of a street cleaner, a windshield wiper, and an automobile motor, respectively. Even if I can't list the names of all the women who have added their intellectual fuel to America's engine of progress, we have to take the time to recognize, in their name, the creativity and ingenuity of our latter-day creators and inventors, many of whom are eloquently heralded in the pages of Cobblestone publications.

Today's young Americans, who represent our newest cycle of intellectual enthusiasm and achievement, are our reminder that America's future security as a nation does not lie in clinging to old technologies or old ways of thinking but in creating new ideas and new technologies that will keep this country competitive into the twenty-first century. Right now a revolution in education is taking place. New ways of creative and inventive thinking are entering curricula around the country. With partnerships among the U.S. Patent and Trademark Office, the U.S. Copyright Office, the National Inventive Thinking Association, the patent attorney associations, the Patent and Trademark Depository Libraries, Centers for the Book, and inventors' organizations, talented teachers across the nation are able to create more challenging courses and broaden their students' minds.

America is depending on you, its youth, to rise to new levels of creative and inventive thinking. We need your know-how because this country is moving into a new age of technology that is going to make the Industrial Revolution look like the Jurassic Age — pretty interesting and pretty obsolete. We are going to need young men and women who understand the concepts of intellectual property so that they have the ability to innovate in the technological industries that are the root of our economic wealth and stability today. We are going to need people who will know how to use, repair, and update systems like the information superhighway President Bill Clinton has talked so much about. If we don't have young people who understand the basics of satellite encryption signals or why copyrights are critically important to selling everything from music videos to computer software, we are going to lose first place in the global marketplace of the twenty-first century.

The land, minerals, and natural resources of this country are finite. At the close of this century, we will no longer be able to depend on them for more wealth for our economic future. But we have something available to us that is far more important and a limitless source of invention. We have the boundless creativity of America's imagination. America's destiny lies in mining the wealth of the human mind.

— Bruce A. Lehman

If only about eight percent of patents granted to Americans in 1993 included the name of a woman, we have certainly wasted a valuable resource. The country — indeed the whole world — is beset with problems that need solving. Some of these problems need to be solved with new, patentable products and processes. Other problems require social inventions that cannot be patented, although they can lead to new ways in which we manage our lives and serve our society. Women and men must participate equally in these problem-solving efforts if we, as a nation and a society, are to work to our full potential.

Most of what we see around us is a product of the human mind. Natural wonders (plants, animals, weather) require human intervention if we are to save our planet as we know it. Human creativity will determine our future. Women's opportunities and responsibilities are equal to those of men.

This book is about opportunity and motivation. Great women, sometimes overcoming enormous social obstacles, have made contributions that have changed our world and continue to change our lives. We examine American history to find women who have invented to make their own lives easier. We examine the lives of living women who have invented for fun and profit. We examine the lives of highly educated women who, as part of their NASA employment, have created inventions that are almost magical in their sophistication. Many of these women tell us about their joys and frustrations.

If you learn about the history of technology, we will be happy. If you learn some skills that enhance creativity, we will be delighted. If you are motivated to become an inventor, we will have achieved our dream. This book is about opportunity. Let each individual become all that she or he is capable of becoming. Let each become a fully functioning human being.

> **Think of creativity as a kind of magic. The inventor is a magician; she or he has learned to fantasize.**

....................

COMPUTERS ARE FUN learning tools because we can touch them, press buttons, play with words and numbers, and even make pictures. They are like living books.

Pretend that this book is alive. Talk to it, write on it, draw pictures with it, let it be your friend — a friend who challenges your mind and stretches your very being. Let it be your partner as you grow, evolve, become.

We begin this book with a make-believe story to tickle your fancy. Think of creativity as a kind of magic. To change your world, *you* must change; *you* must become a new person with a new perspective on life; *you* must dare to pretend. Dare to say "what if ?" The inventor is a magician; she or he has learned to fantasize.

Our stories from history are true, but they also are fantastic, as they describe how women created the unexpected. Our stories about living women are magical. Each of the women started as a little girl who played with ideas, became a student — more serious but still willing to toy with ideas — and grew up to become an inventor. Some adults become rigid and unimaginative in their thinking. Not so for the women in this book.

The activity sections are important. They are designed so that teachers can use the book in cross-curriculum studies. Many of them relate to science and technology, while also tying in with mathematics, language arts, aesthetics (art and music), literature, and social studies.

The activities provide for different types of learning and for students at different levels. Some students will want to start with hands-on activities and use those as the basis for their reading and writing exercises. Other activities are challenging to students who excel at reading, writing, and research through the printed word. Some projects are set out in a particular order, but students may want to approach them in a different way, jumping in at a point that most interests them.

The activity sections allow students to get involved in the book with their whole being — mind and body. We hope that you won't hold back. Believe in yourself. Trust in yourself. This book is about women who believed in themselves — even when they had to risk exploring a new idea. Let the women herein act as role models to help you dare to think of new ideas.

To prepare for activities suggested in different chapters, you might want to spend some time gathering items that you can use in various inventing exercises. Some suggested items include mousetraps; springs; nails, nuts, and bolts; wheels; skates; skateboards; pencil sharpeners; paper punches; small fans; wire; coat hangers; containers; spools; aluminum foil; bubble wrap; loose packing material such as Styrofoam "peanuts."

At the end of the book are some helpful hints, additional resources, and a bibliography. This book is, after all, not the end of the road you must travel to reach the U.S. Patent Office. Instead, it should point you in the right direction.

An important feature for students and teachers is the definitions sprinkled throughout the text. Words set in boldface in the text are defined in the margin. These definitions will help expand students' vocabulary and prevent confusion, especially concerning scientific terms.

A final word about boys and men: In this book, we tell stories about women and try to encourage girls because they are underrepresented as inventors. But we want to encourage boys as well. After all, we need everyone's talents. Men and women working together in a mutually supportive environment is a goal toward which we should all strive.

# THE SPINNER

*A Fairy Tale Never Told*

Once there was a beautiful maiden kept prisoner in a glass box. She looked out at the world from all sides. People brought her food and were kind. She kept busy spinning the wool and linen people supplied. They took her thread and made wonderful things out of it.

Gradually, the glass began splintering. The girl gathered up the shards and spun it into thread. People came and said, "Why aren't you working? You're just playing." They could not see the glass.

She said, "I am spinning what is around me."

They thought she had gone mad. Many people came to look at the girl who they thought was spinning nothing. They would not bring her food because they did not want to reward her for spinning nothing.

After a while, most of the glass had been spun. All that was left was the locked door. Her keepers thought she was still in a glass prison and kept coming through the door, just as before.

She was getting hungry, and she had to do something with the glass thread — it was taking up too much space. So she knit it into walls. Her box looked just like it had before. But since she had spun and knit it herself, she knew how to unravel the walls. She could get out if she wanted to.

But what would she eat on the outside? And where would she live? Once again, she began spinning the wool, linen, and other fibers people brought her. The people also brought her food and decided she had regained her senses.

But the spinner's life was boring. She asked them to bring her blue dye, saying it was for the wool. She unraveled her glass walls, dyed the thread blue, and reknit it. She knit it so fine that it went much further and she was able to add new rooms. Now all her walls were blue.

People came from afar to see the girl who was kept in a lovely blue prison. She had never attracted any notice before because the walls had been transparent. Visitors thought she was just a girl sitting and spinning, free as anyone. Now they were outraged. "Why do you keep a girl in a prison?" they asked. "What has she done? Let her out!"

Her keepers said, "We aren't the ones who built her prison! It was just our job to keep her there! Anyway, she was crazy. But she seems all right now. She can come and go as she pleases."

Soon all the people wanted blue glass houses, and the girl earned enough money to travel throughout the world. Some say she transformed herself into mist and reappears as a beautiful woman at dawn, when she beckons young girls who are awake to follow her.

1

# GOING

WHO WERE THE FIRST WOMEN inventors in America? No one knows for sure. What we do know is that early American settlers had to be extremely inventive to survive and to build communities in a land of forests. Machinery and tools had to be brought across the sea or made at home. The success of the colonies depended on the creativity of all the settlers — men and women.

This fact gave women more of a chance to develop talents not usually considered womanly. In the early 1600s and 1700s, women operated shops, inns, farms, and mills. They learned trades usually thought of as "men's work." But as the colonies grew, women's roles became more restricted. Men formed governments modeled on those of the "old countries" in Europe. In the eyes of the law in these societies, a woman was seen as a man's mother, wife, or child — not as an individual in her own right. Except in cases of dire need, she was expected to center her activities on the home. Therefore, the history of women inventors is also the history of women's changing role in society.

## AN AGE-OLD HELPER

Falling water has been used since the earliest civilizations as a source of power. Water wheels were used in early America for grinding grain to make flour, to power sawmills, and to do other work. Wheels were

# Against the Stream

and to do other work. Wheels were made from wood, with wooden buckets, floats, or paddles attached to the rim. Often they were near natural waterfalls. The falling water was directed into or against the buckets or paddles, forcing the wheel to turn down into the stream, where the buckets caught water and kept the wheel going. Especially in later years, dams were often built to provide falling water for a mill and to create a reservoir of water that could be tapped when needed.

In 1700, Pennsylvania colonists used a water wheel to grind Indian corn brought in from the fields. But the distance from the mill to customers in Philadelphia made it a risky business. Even so, planter Thomas Masters and his wife, Sybilla, bought Governor's Mill in 1714. How could they convince other colonists to use their gristmill and not one closer to their homes? Her answer: Produce a better, finer quality of flour. How to do this? Improve the machinery used in cleaning and processing grain.

◆ OPPOSITE AND ABOVE: Today, near streams in the countryside, quaint old mills with water wheels are found. They once provided the energy that made commerce and industry possible in America.

In the usual gristmill operation, the job of the large water wheel was to turn one heavy millstone on top of another so as to crush and grind grains such as corn and wheat. Conveying the movement of the water wheel to the top millstone required several devices. The colonists used large oak shafts, stone bearings, and wooden gears, pinions, and cogwheels to connect the water wheel to the millstone and make the stone move with the wheel.

Sybilla Masters's invention used the same machinery except that instead of using a millstone to grind the corn, she used pestles, or mallets, which were raised up and down to crush the grain. Power, according to Sybilla, could be supplied either by "beasts of burden," such as horses and oxen, or by the traditional water wheel.

Sybilla apparently had observed Tuscarora Indian women making "Tuscarora rice." This was a food similar to hominy that was made from corn. The process removed the hull, or outside covering, and ground the corn into a powder that could be easily cooked or baked. Instead of grinding their corn with a flat stone, the women placed the grain in a large bowl and beat it with a pestle.

Sybilla adapted this technology by inventing a kind of stamping machine, so that the corn was crushed by an up-and-down movement of a mallet. According to Sybilla, the end product was "easy to transport" and good for treating illnesses such as "consumption," a common name given to chronic illnesses, especially diseases of the lungs, such as tuberculosis, that caused people gradually to grow weaker.

## A WOMAN OF MANY TALENTS

The Masters family did not depend entirely on farming and milling for a living. Sybilla also found time, between field and home chores, to make hats. So did other colonists. She needed to give people a reason to buy hers. Her answer: Invent a way to make a new, more attractive hat.

Then as now, it was not enough to have good ideas. To succeed in business, a person had to protect her or his rights to profit from an invention. There was no U.S. patent law to keep others from using a new technique; there was only English law. (See Appendix 1 for a discussion of U.S. patents.) Inventors wishing government protection to keep others from using their ideas could apply to King George for a document, called a patent, granting protection. This document could be shown if there was any argument about rights in either the mother country or its colonies.

Sybilla must have been courageous, confident, and ambitious. Around 1712, she boarded a ship bound for England, armed with drawings and descriptions of her new ideas. After arriving in England, she had to convince the king's lawyers of the value of her work. She also had to answer many technical questions and prove that she had invented the techniques herself.

She came home a few years later with a patent granted to her husband, Thomas, for "A New Invencon found out by Sybilla, his Wife, for Cleaning and Curing the Indian Corn Growing in the severall Colonies in America." Sybilla received another patent, also granted to Thomas, for "A New Way of Working and Staining in Straw, and the Platt and Leaf of the Palmeta Tree, and covering and Adorning Hatt and Bonnett, in such a Manner as was never before Done or Practised in England or Any of our Plantacons." These documents gave the couple "full power, sole privilege and authority" to profit from the inventions wherever England ruled.

*Hat making was an important industry in early America. Women played an important role as designers and makers.*

While Sybilla was away, Thomas had built a mill in Philadelphia based on her new method of cleaning and drying grain. On her return, they began a profitable business.

We wish we knew more about Sybilla Masters's background. It's not so surprising that she devised new methods for hat making. But how did she become familiar with machinery and mechanical drawings?

Sybilla's father was a mariner and merchant who owned a plantation on the banks of the Delaware River. Most of what the family needed was made on the plantation. There were seven children in the family. Perhaps Sybilla was the one who showed the most interest in mechanical things, and so knowledge was passed on to her.

## NOT IN HER NAME

Why were Sybilla Masters's patents granted in her husband's name if she was the admitted inventor? At that time, a married woman's property legally belonged to her husband. In addition, it was conventional in England, and for a long time in America, for men to act on behalf of female relatives in business matters. Men were responsible for protecting their wives and sisters and for seeing that they were treated justly.

Thus, Sybilla Masters must have been quite a surprise to the king's lawyers in England. They may have wondered why Thomas had sent his wife to petition the king for patents. But Sybilla no doubt knew that she would be the best person to explain the workings of her new devices. And she must have convinced them that she was the true inventor, for the patent reads "found out by Sybilla."

As the social order in America became more established, it became more difficult for women who showed an interest in machines or other technology to be taken seriously. Women were educated differently than men. During the eighteenth and nineteenth centuries, and for much of the twentieth century, women were trained in the manners and morals of polite society and in the care of the home and children. People considered a woman "educated" if she could discuss art, literature, and current events in an intelligent, informed way. Men studied science, technology,

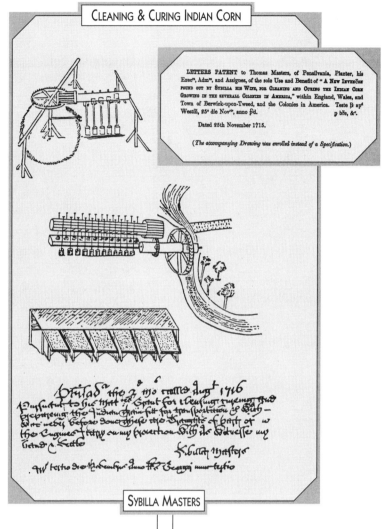

CLEANING & CURING INDIAN CORN

LETTERS PATENT to Thomas Masters, of Pensilvania, Planter, his Exec.^rs, Adm.^rs, and Assignes, of the sole Use and Benefit of "A New Invencõn found out by Sibylla his Wife, for Cleaning and Curing the Indian Corn Growing in the severall Colonies in America," within England, Wales, and Town of Berwick-upon-Tweed, and the Colonies in America. Teste B. ap.^d Westm̃, 25° die Nov.^r, anno Ð̃d. p b̃re, &.^c.

Dated 25th November 1715.

*(The accompanying Drawing was enrolled instead of a Specification.)*

SYBILLA MASTERS

◆ Sybilla Masters may have adapted her invention from a technique used by the Tuscarora Indians, who had come to Pennsylvania after losing a great conflict in North Carolina.

and the art of politics.

Social pressures prevented many women from stepping out of traditional women's roles. A woman inventor needed the self-confidence to ignore being called unwomanly, or even immoral, for going against tradition.

## HATS OFF TO HAT MAKERS

When the U.S. Patent Office was established in 1790, it set up no specific barriers to women. Yet few women could afford to hire a lawyer to help with the legal requirements of filing a patent or technicians to help with drawings or models.

When women finally did begin applying for patents, most often they were for new methods of making clothing, including hats. Women in many New England communities earned good money converting straw into hats. This involved cutting, boiling, dyeing, flattening, splitting, braiding, and bleaching the straw fibers. One hat maker, Betsey Metcalf, invented a popular new method of braiding straw in 1798. She made this comment in a letter to her sister: "Many said I ought to get a patent; but I told them I did not wish to have my name sent to Congress." Apparently, Metcalf felt it was improper for a modest woman to call such attention to herself. A woman had to be a bit radical to press ahead and demand recognition for her work and abilities.

Hat maker Mary Kies was somewhat bolder and became the first woman to apply for and receive a U.S. patent. It was granted in 1809 for a process for weaving straw with silk or thread. Kies was praised by First Lady Dolley Madison for boosting the nation's hat industry. Unfortunately, the patent documents showing the process were destroyed in the great Patent Office fire of 1836.

By the year 1841, women held twenty-two patents, mostly related to clothing. After that, women tinkerers began applying for patents for all kinds of gadgets and devices related to the work they did.

## EASING THEIR BURDEN

During the 1800s, most women's lives were filled with long, hard hours milking cows, skimming milk, churning butter, washing, cooking, and cleaning. Of course, they also gave birth to children, tried to raise them properly, and often worked in the fields. If a woman took time to invent something new, it was usually a way to ease her burden or make money from her labors.

Typical inventions by women were churns for making butter, beekeeping equipment, and improved cook stoves. Women received patents

◆ Women took an active part in the important hat-making industry in early America. In 1809, Mary Kies became the first woman to receive a patent from the U.S. Patent Office, granted for a technique of weaving straw with silk or thread.

for feminine hygiene and birth control devices. One woman, Anna Corey Baldwin of Newark, New Jersey, the wife of a dairy farmer, received four patents between 1869 and 1879 for inventions that had to do with milk.

Baldwin's first invention was for using milk in other useful products. She boiled milk, skimmed off the bone marrow that floated to the top, and eliminated all moisture from the marrow. The result was a substance that could be used as an ointment or for slicking back hair.

Another patented technique was a way to make a sweet alcoholic drink, or cordial, and a vinegar from milk. Baldwin let some milk sit until it curdled and produced a clear liquid, or whey. She added brown sugar to the whey and let the mixture ferment (a chemical process caused by the sugar). If she used about one pound of sugar to six quarts of whey, the result was an excellent cordial. About one pound of sugar to sixteen quarts of whey resulted in a vinegar.

Baldwin also invented a milk cooler. She inserted a tube filled with ice or cold water into a large container of milk. Paddles attached to the lid of the container could be agitated to stir and cool the milk quickly.

The last invention for which Baldwin received a patent was for an improvement in suction milking machines. She called it the Hygienic Glove Milker. Her device was a rubber cover that fitted over the cow's udder, with rubber tubes that fitted over the teats. These attached to a larger tube that was connected to a suction pump.

We do not know whether Baldwin ever earned any money from these inventions.

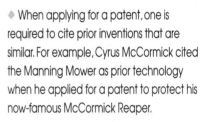

◆ When applying for a patent, one is required to cite prior inventions that are similar. For example, Cyrus McCormick cited the Manning Mower as prior technology when he applied for a patent to protect his now-famous McCormick Reaper.

## HIDDEN FOREVER

Many women let others take the credit for their ideas. A Patent Office publication titled *From Buttons to Biotech* states, "At one time it was not uncommon in the United States for a man to receive a patent for an invention that was actually invented by a woman, typically his wife."

In 1843, William Manning received a patent for an "improvement in grass and grain cutting machines." According to the literature of the time, Manning gave credit for the invention to his wife, Ann Harned Manning. Later, Cyrus McCormick made further improvements and became famous for his McCormick Reaper, a machine that made harvesting grain much more efficient.

Some women did get patents for farm machinery in their own names.

THE MANNING MOWER

Anna Trexler, of Minnesota, patented the Combined Plow and Harrow (1888), and Lucy Easton, also of Minnesota, received a patent for the Flaxseed Separating Machine (1890).

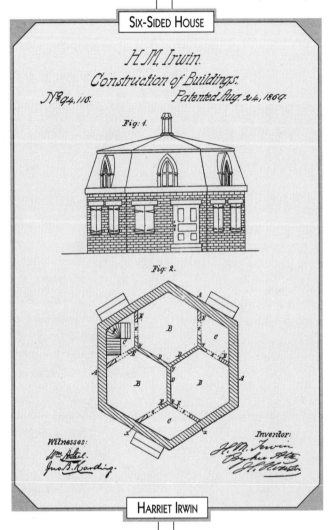

SIX-SIDED HOUSE

HARRIET IRWIN

## IF A WOMAN'S PLACE IS IN THE HOME . . .

Home design was off-limits to women because it involved architecture and the building trades. But what could interest a woman more than the design of a house? Harriet Irwin, a North Carolina woman born in 1828, never took formal courses in design and construction or worked in these areas. Yet she was deeply interested in architecture and how the design of a house related to the way people lived.

In 1869, "H.I. Irwin" (she may have tried to hide the fact that she was a woman) received a patent for the Improvement in Construction of Houses. Her design was for a six-sided, or hexagonal, house that was not only beautiful but also easy to care for and keep comfortable all year long.

She said in the patent, "The objects of my invention are the economizing of space and building materials, the obtaining of economical heating mediums, thorough lighting and ventilation, and facilities for inexpensive ornamentation." In other words, her design dealt with these questions: Did the house make the most efficient use of space? Would it cost very much to build? Would it cost much to keep at a comfortable temperature? Could it be beautiful but not expensive?

Irwin's was not the first six-sided house, but it had many new features. She eliminated hallways, considering them a waste of space. The rooms connected to each other so that people could move easily between them. The way they fitted together inside the hexagonal design provided more space than a square or rectangular house of the same length.

An efficient heating system was one of her goals. Irwin placed a chimney at the point where the walls of two rooms met. She put in flues from the chimney to connect with fireplaces in other rooms. The placement of windows helped keep air moving throughout the house in nice weather.

Irwin was born Harriet Morrison, daughter of Robert Hall Morrison, the founder and first president of Davidson College in North Carolina. He believed strongly that women should receive higher education. Yet the school where he sent his three daughters, the Institution for Female Education in Salem, North Carolina (which became Salem College), did not teach young ladies about architecture or building. Harriet had to learn about these subjects through her own reading and independent study. She kept up this interest after her marriage, at age twenty, to a well-to-do cotton manufacturer, James Irwin.

Even though Harriet Irwin had many advantages, her life was not easy. She had always been frail, yet she had nine babies, five of whom lived beyond infancy. When the Civil War raged in North Carolina, the family suffered many hardships.

After the war, Irwin built a two-story frame house with a mansard roof and a central tower, based on her own design. She lived in it and designed other, similar houses. Her husband and brother-in-law formed a business to build and sell her houses.

Irwin kept up her passion for reading and wrote numerous articles about the Colonial and Revolutionary periods in America. She also wrote a novel called *The Hermit of Petraea*. It is about a man who goes to live in a far-off region of the world. The man enters a hexagonal house that fills him with delight. "The soul of the artist spoke in every line and curve, projection and recess," the narrator says. "And the effect of the whole was as magically beautiful as though built by a painter's brush."

Irwin died in 1897, but her house stood in Charlotte, North Carolina, for one hundred years. One year the porch was lopped off to make room for a highway. Sometime after 1963, the house was razed to make way for development.

Irwin's 1869 patent brought the total number of U.S. patents to 94,116 (her patent number). Out of these, about 440 were held by women. Because of her courage, Irwin helped usher in a new era for women inventors.

> *Harriet Irwin showed much courage when she entered the male-dominated world of architecture to design and supervise the building of her dream house.*

# ACTIVITIES

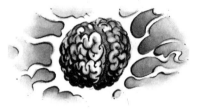

## *Project 1*

## YOU ARE AN INVENTOR

### Objective

Students will be asked to brainstorm as part of several activities in this book. The following exercise allows them to practice the technique as it relates to inventing.

Inventors often use brainstorming to help them solve problems. Review the following procedure and get ready to invent.

**1. Brainstorm problems.** Look around. What needs improving? What bugs you? What causes problems for people? What is hard to use? List at least fifteen problems.

☞ Examples: My school desk gets messy. I don't have enough space in my room. I get thirsty in class. I find it hard to find things in my locker. Students don't have enough voice in school decisions.

I hate the hard kernels in popcorn.

**2. Make a selection.** Choose a problem from your list. Pick one that you would really like to solve. Write down a few thoughts about the problem. Don't worry if you don't have a solution. That's the point. It wouldn't be a problem if you knew the solution.

☞ Example: My locker is a mess. The biggest problem is that I never know how to make sure that I leave stuff I don't need at home in school — and that I take home what I need for homework and Scouts.

**3. Brainstorm ideas.** List all the solutions you can think of — at least thirty. Write crazy ideas as well as practical ones. Don't judge! Way-out ideas might trigger useful ideas later. Boring ideas might lead you to exciting places.

☞ Examples: Paint everything in a take-home color and a leave-at-school color. Build drawers and more shelves in my locker. Use stick-on labels. Ask for two lockers. Leave stuff on top of the locker. Build shelves inside the door (like those inside a refrigerator).

Now really stretch your mind. Try

for twenty more ideas. "Free-wheeling" is welcome.

☞ Examples: Dig an extra space below my locker. Dig into the wall behind my locker for extra space. Bring an extra locker from home that fits on top of my locker. Throw away half the stuff in my locker. Hire an assistant to remember what I should bring home. Make lists inside the door.

**4. Combine and improve.** When you think you have exhausted your ideas, try to create more ideas by changing or combining those already listed. Each modification counts as another idea.

☞ Examples: Paint shelves different colors. Instead of an extra locker on top, I can hang an extra locker on the door.

**5. Judge the ideas.** Select one of the ideas, or a combination of them, that appeals to you. Expand on it as much as possible. Brainstorm additional ideas to make it work.

☞ Example: I'd like to combine several options: Build drawers and more shelves in the locker. Build shelves inside the door (like those inside a refrigerator). Bring an extra locker from home that fits on top of my locker. What I want to do is design an insert for my locker (a locker within my locker) where I could keep things that I have to take home. The insert would be made of a hard plastic material (like a hard-sided suitcase). Perhaps it could hang on the inside of the locker door. It would have a handle like a suitcase, as well as straps, so that I could wear it. I would put take-home stuff into the "suitcase locker." At the end of the day, I would remove the insert and carry the whole thing home. It would fit on my closet door at home and act as an insert locker in my closet.

**6. Stretch.** It's time for a final burst of creativity. Brainstorm five ways in which you can improve your invention.

☞ Examples: I will mold the "suitcase locker" so that it fits my back comfortably. I will decorate the outside with school colors and a picture of the mascot. This item will have a built-in combination (the same number as my locker combination) for protection and easy remembering. My locker will stay more orderly because I will use the insert only for items that go home. At home, it will remind me to take the appropriate items to school.

**7. Do it!** Make your product — or make a model of your invention. Explore the idea with classmates. Do they like the idea? Might they buy it? What improvements do they suggest? How might you market your invention? Perhaps you're

already on your way to becoming a millionaire.

**8. Discussion.** If you worked in a group, was it hard to share "crazy" ideas? What was fun about the project? Did some bizarre ideas prove to be helpful? Was it interesting to see how other students added to your idea? Were you protective about your invention — your baby?

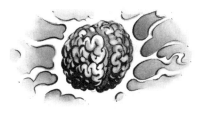

## Project 2
## DESIGN A HAT CONTEST

### Objective
A hands-on exercise in creativity and imagination, with the challenge of finding different uses for ordinary materials.

This activity will give you a chance to use your head in more ways than one. The idea is to design a hat the likes of which has never been seen before! Contestants can be individuals or small groups.

**1. Decide on the purpose of the hat.** Whom is it for? A princess, a magician, a construction worker, a teacher, a shy person, a dandy? Will it be for winter or summer? Will it do something practical or funny, or will it just sit on the head? Will it attract attention? Will it provide protection?

To spark ideas, look at this list of kinds of hats:

☞ hardhats, to protect construction workers

☞ crowns, to signify royalty

☞ a witch's or wizard's hat to add mysterious powers

☞ a magician's hat, to help with tricks

☞ a sunbonnet, to protect the face

☞ a ski cap, to protect the face and head

Add at least five other kinds of hats to the list, noting each one's purpose. Look at other continents for ideas. Do Asian and African hats suggest innovations?

**2. Construction ideas.** To prepare for this activity, bring in some different kinds of hats and study the construction. Then gather or consider the different kinds of tools or materials you might need, such as needles, staples, glue, and various kinds of paper and fabric.

You might want to start out by making a headband out of construction paper or some other flexible material and use that to build on. You could attach soft fabric to it, then stiffen it and give it shape with another material inside. Ask these questions: What shape? How high? Will it be stiff or soft and floppy? What materials will I use for the inside, to give it shape? What do I want for the outside? Something beautiful and shiny? Warm? Cool?

☞ Some materials that you might use include the following: aluminum foil (for shaping or for a shiny effect), felt, ribbon, string, leather, plain and fancy fabrics, cardboard (both stiff and flexible), Styrofoam, and wire

**3. Something different.** What special and different effect could your hat have? Say it is for a dressmaker, a tailor, or a hat maker (milliner). What are some of her or his special needs? A place to put pins so they are always near? A place to keep a measuring tape? Other needs?

If the hat is for a magician, how big should it be? Should it have a secret compartment? Could it be two or three hats in one? What needs do magicians have?

**4. Vote.** Ask students from another class to be the judges. Give prizes for the funniest, most practical, most complicated, most beautiful, and silliest hats, as well as the one most likely to become popular. Be certain that everyone wins a prize.

*Puzzle 1*

## CAN YOU SOLVE THE RIDDLES?

Riddles require a slightly different way of looking at things — and that is a talent important to inventors!

1. What can be stolen yet never touched? (Read about Sybilla Masters.)

2. When does an inventor become a "hidden inventor," even though she or he might be standing in plain sight? (Read "Hidden Forever.")

3. Who invented the following:

   **a.** A way to make the hair behave

   **b.** A whey for adventuresome eating

   **c.** A way to keep the white stuff cool

   **d.** A way to milk while reading

(Read "Easing Their Burden.")

**Answers on page 159.**

*Puzzle 2*

## NOW WHAT DID THEY MEAN BY THAT?

**Objective**
An examination of the meaning of words and how words can be used literally or figuratively. This exercise should follow a discussion of water mills and how they operated.

1. "Show me your metal" is a common saying. What do we mean when we say it? What early technology would you guess it comes from? Write three possible original meanings of the phrase. Make up anything that sounds possible!

2. "Keep your nose to the grindstone" is another saying we use today. How would you explain what it means? As you might guess, it is related to water mills. How did the saying originate? Give three possible meanings before looking at the answer.

3. In these sayings, words are used in a nonliteral sense. When someone says, "Show me your metal," she or he does not expect you to find some metal you own and show

it to her or him. Another saying using words in a nonliteral way is "penny pincher." When we call someone a penny pincher, we don't mean the person actually pinches pennies. We mean that she or he hates to spend money. Can you think of other examples of words or sayings used in a nonliteral sense?

**Answers on page 159.**

*Puzzle 3*

## THE RIGHT WORDS

Cross out the incorrect words or phrases in the following sentences. More than one word or phrase might be correct.

**1.** There were more men than women inventors in early America because of differences in education / work experience / legal rights / tradition / natural aptitude / seriousness / intelligence. (Read "Not in Her Name.")

**2.** During Colonial days, many women in New England made hats out of straw. The fibers had to be dyed / flattened / cut / split / braided / bleached / boiled. (Read "Hats Off to Hat Makers.")

**3.** Betsey Metcalf invented a popular new method of braiding straw in 1798. She did not apply for a patent because she was too poor / uneducated / modest / confused / threatened / busy.

**4.** By the year 1841, women held twenty-two patents, mostly related to cleaning house / health problems / farm work / child care / clothing.

**Answers on page 159.**

*Think About It*

### Objective
Students gain perspective about their world by comparing conditions of the past with those of the present.

**1.** Conditions have changed a great deal for women since Colonial days. Are there any legal restrictions today on what women or men can do based on their gender? Can you think of any ways in which society makes it difficult for a woman or a man to use her or his talents? (Some suggestions might be stereotyping about what is suitable for a boy/man or a girl/woman to do; laws restricting men's and women's roles, such as in the military.)

**2.** In the nineteenth century, Anna Corey Baldwin invented a way to make a thick substance from boiled milk that could be used as an ointment or for slicking back hair. Milk was the first product, produced by cows. The ointment was a "byproduct," or secondary product. Almost everything people make is a byproduct of something else. What is made from sawdust? List all the things you can think of that are made from wood. You might think of this as a "recycling" challenge.

**3.** During the nineteenth century, more complex turbine engines were developed to use waterpower. Look up the definition of "turbine" and locate pictures of various turbines. What are some ways in which they are used today? You might want to make a drawing of a turbine to illustrate how it works.

**4.** Waterpower systems are looking more and more attractive for the future. Why? Consider: Does waterpower pollute? Is it costly? Is it renewable? Is it efficient, compared to coal- or oil-fueled generating plants?

**5.** What important issues did Harriet Irwin have to worry about in designing and building her dream home? What important issues do home designers and builders today have to address that Irwin did not have to worry about?

## The Way You See It

### Objective

Suggestions for writing assignments. To encourage students to think independently about events in history and how they relate to today. To encourage students to do outside reading, as in finding examples of other independent women in early America.

1. Another Colonial woman who might have sympathized with Sybilla Masters was Abigail Adams. Who was she, and what do you think the two women might have had in common? What might they have said to each other? Join with a partner to write a dialogue. You could each pretend to be one of the characters and ask each other questions. Then write the questions and answers as a dialogue that another student pair could perform.

2. Women have sought legal rights equal to those of men on the basis of what is just in human relations. They have resisted having their abilities defined according to their gender. Make a list of gender-based rules that you think are unfair. How could you change them?

3. Inventions change. The first har-vesting machines were followed by better ones based on the earlier technology. Choose an invention, such as the automobile, airplane, or sewing machine, and follow its development from the first model to the most recent one. Note improvements made. Were some things dropped that you think should have been kept? What improvements could still be made?

4. What might be some differences between designing a home for the country and designing a home for the city?

5. If you were building a house today, what kinds of things might you have to invent to create your ideal home? If you could invent a new material for the outside of a house, what are some of the qualities it would have? What qualities would you want in a new material for the inside?

## Imagine That!

### Objective

To learn by doing, with cross-curriculum application. Preparation includes reading and discussing the chapter sections about the inventors or inventions mentioned.

**1. A cooperative learning activity.** Join with several people to perform a skit in which Sybilla Masters comes before the king of England's lawyers, claiming that she was the inventor of a new way of processing corn. The king's men do not question her about how the contraption works. She has already told them and shown them her drawings. But they do not believe that she invented it herself. "After all, what could a woman know about such things?" they ask. [The teacher might expand on this, suggesting different roles that young people might take.]

**2. A continuing activity.** [Students combine history lessons with learning technology through doing. The result might be a construction project that could be exhibited and used to demonstrate the principles of construction in a lower-grade classroom.]

☞ Visit an old water mill that is still working. Study the way it operates. How many different mechanical devices are used? If no water mill is located nearby, find pictures that illustrate the principles.

☞ As a class, construct a water wheel. What could you use for the wheel? (Possibilities: an existing wheel; one made of cardboard.) What would you use for the buckets, or paddles, that catch the water? (Consider: construction board; metal or plastic that can be bent and shaped; existing objects.) How could you attach the paddles to the wheel? Where would the water come from? What could you use for a shaft? Make sure that when the wheel turns, it also turns the shaft, to which another wheel can be attached. If you carry the idea on, the other wheel would have gears that would engage yet another wheel.

**3. Field trip or resource person.** Hydroelectric power uses the power of falling water to generate electricity. Do you know of any small, modern hydroelectric plants in your region? If so, visit one and ask for a guided tour. Or invite an expert in the field of energy use to class to talk about hydroelectric power. Then write a paper explaining how these plants operate.

**4. Design project.** Design a house with a nontraditional shape. Harriet Irwin built a house around the desire for it to be economical, convenient, and beautiful. She used a six-sided shape.

☞ What would be some of the advantages of this design? What might be some disadvantages?

☞ Make a model of a house with a three-sided shape and note the problems the shape might cause and the advantages it would have.

☞ Try other shapes. Brainstorm ideas and answers.

**5. A cooperative learning activity.** Plan an ideal house. As a class, form three groups: one all boys, one all girls, and one with both boys and girls. Have each group plan a house. How do the plans

differ? What were the reasons for the designs?

**6. Design project.** Design a sign that might have hung outside a Colonial hat shop. Remember, many people did not know how to read. In Colonial times, signs were of interesting shapes, designs, and colors to catch the eye and give a sense of the merchandise sold. In some regions, historians have re-created Colonial towns, using wonderful old signs. If possible, visit these places for ideas. Or look at pictures and read articles about Colonial Williamsburg or other early American towns.

Develop sign designs for a shoemaker, a tailor, a hat maker, a blacksmith, and a doctor. What other businesses or professions of the Colonial period can you think of?

**7. Brainstorming.** Inventors are people who look at old things in new ways. How many uses can you think of for a banana peel? Brainstorm!

☞ Form two groups. Have one group list and describe some uses for the banana peel. Have the other group draw, cartoon style if they wish, ideas they have for the peel. For example, use a banana peel for an ant umbrella.

☞ Try the same activity for an orange peel. What else might we "recycle" into something fun or useful?

*You Say Yes; I Say No*

**Objective**
Topics for debate.

**1.** Ever since the U.S. Patent Office was established in 1790, it has treated men and women equally. Yet few women applied for patents in the early days, and men's names still far outnumber women's names on patents. This is evidence that women are not as inventive as men. Do you agree or disagree?

**2.** With a few exceptions, women in the early nineteenth century were granted patents for devices relating to the female sphere of activity, such as churns for making butter, while men's patents were more often for machinery and devices used in industry. This could mean that women and men are born with different abilities. Or it could mean that creative people, whether men or women, tend to solve problems relating to their own everyday lives. Which do you believe is true?

# 2

# IRONS IN

THE CIVIL WAR (1861–1865) MARKED A turning point for women inventors. The war called men away from farms, shops, and factories, leaving women to carry on. If a plow or another piece of farm equipment broke down, the woman had to repair it. In many cases, the woman not only had children to take care of but also was responsible for the family business. If there were decisions to be made about buying or selling, trading or borrowing, she made them. These experiences built confidence in women. Many discovered that they were handy with machines and adept at solving problems that involved technology.

During the war, the slaves were freed. After it, black men were given the right to vote. This encouraged women to seek the same right for themselves and to insist on more freedom to develop and use their talents.

When the war was over, men and many women had a desire to get back to normal. But the record was clear: When women were needed to do "men's work," they did it well. During the next seventy years, the number of women applying for patents gradually increased. Many hoped to earn income from their inventions and gain more control over their lives. Their inventions included devices for the home, industry, water conservation, and war.

## HELPING WITH THE WAR

During the Civil War, not all of women's inventions were for the workaday world. Mechanically talented women on both sides of the Civil War did what they could to help their side win. However, Confederate women would have had trouble getting a patent for an invention through the U.S. Patent Office. The records we have are those of women who sided with the Union.

One of the inventions that related directly to the war effort was the Underwater Telescope by Sarah Mather, of New York. The device for "locating and studying underwater objects" was first patented in 1845.

# THE FIRE

When the war broke out, Mather made improvements in it so that Union submarines could use her telescope to gather information. (Both the Union and the Confederacy used several submarines during the Civil War.) The patent document provides this description: "The nature of my invention consists in constructing a tube with a lamp attached to one end thereof so as to be sunk in the water to illuminate objects therein, and a telescope to view said objects and make examinations under water."

*The most popular "sad iron" ever produced was invented by Mary F. Potts in 1870. The iron became known as "Mrs. Potts' Cold Handle Sad Iron" — the greatest innovation until the electric iron.*

Also relating to battles fought on water was Temperance P. Edson's Self-Inflator, a device for raising up boats that had sunk.

Clarissa Britain, of Michigan, received patents for seven inventions. One 1863 patent was for an Improvement in Ambulances. It was used to transport wounded men from the battlefield to a hospital without having to move them from a stretcher.

Martha Coston, of Washington, D.C., had been married to an inventor who had died and left her with four small children and little money. Fortunately, she had taken a great interest in his work, especially a system of sending signals at night through pyrotechnics, or fireworks. She sought the advice of pyrotechnics experts and developed a system of codes using different colors. During the Civil War, she sold the rights to her Improvements in Pyrotechnical Night Signals to the U.S. government for twenty thousand dollars. She also received a contract to build the flares. In an early version of the pyrotechnic night signal patent, Martha is listed as "administratrix of the last will and testament of B. Franklin Coston, deceased." She later received a patent for her own improvements of the device.

Yours Truly

M, Florence Potts

INVENTRESS OF MRS. POTTS' COLD HANDLE SAD IRON.

## THE WORLD OF WORK

### Sad Irons

Keeping clothes and house linens clean and pressed was a particularly hard job for women in the days before easy-care fabrics and washing machines. Before the electric iron was invented, people used heavy irons made of solid iron and heated on a stove. These were called "sad irons." The irons themselves were not sad, but the women and girls who sweated over the ironing board certainly were! Actually, the word "sad" also meant heavy.

A terrible problem with ironing was that the iron's handle also became hot. Early handles were made of iron, which conducted heat from the base. Once handles were made of wood, that problem was solved. But because heat rises, the heat from the hot base would radiate up and burn the knuckles of a woman who was ironing. Women often would wrap a rag around their knuckles for protection.

The most popular "sad iron" ever produced was invented by Mary F. Potts in 1870. Her father was a plasterer, so she had special knowledge about that material. She thought that if the central part of the iron were plaster, it would be lighter and cooler on the knuckles. She built a plaster mold and took it to a local foundry, or ironworking shop, and had a thin layer of iron put on the sides and a heavier layer put on the bottom, where it was needed to hold the heat and to press the fabric. Potts made her iron double-pointed so that it could be used in either direction.

Potts also figured out a way to keep the bottom of an iron hot at all times and still have a cool handle. Her popular invention was a set of three bases with one removable handle. While one iron base was being used, the other two could be kept hot on the stove. When the one being used cooled down, the ironer simply switched to one of the hot ones, snapping on the cool handle. The iron became known as "Mrs. Potts' Cold Handle Sad Iron" — the greatest innovation until the electric iron.

### Sewing Machines

Women have long worked in factories, especially in the garment-making and fabric industries. They also have been the primary sewers at home, often making all the family's clothes

◆ ABOVE: An advertisement from the late 1800s tells the advantages of inventor Mary Florence Potts's new iron.

◆ BELOW: Helen Blanchard received twenty-four patents, mostly for improvements on sewing machines or attachments. Shown here is a patent model of one of her machines, which she sold through her own company.

*It is not surprising that several women inventors have made improvements in sewing-related machinery and methods.*

...........................

and linens. It is not surprising that several women inventors have made improvements in sewing-related machinery and methods.

Helen Blanchard was the daughter of a prominent shipbuilder in Maine. She probably would never have become an inventor if her father's business had not failed. But when he died, she was left with expensive tastes and no money. Fortunately for her, she was not only mechanically talented but also persistent.

She began tinkering with sewing machines, figuring out improvements that would be "new and useful" and earn her money. She had to borrow money for her first patent application fee. But she had faith in herself and did not stop with one improvement. Blanchard's first patent, granted in 1873, was followed by twenty-three others, mostly for improvements on sewing machines or attachments. One of her devices sewed and trimmed knitted fabrics in one operation. The modern zigzag machine is based partly on her earlier technology.

Blanchard developed a company to market her inventions — The American Buttonhole, Overseaming and Sewing Machine Company. She did so well on royalties from the use of her inventions and from her own business that she was able to buy back the family homestead, which had been lost when her father's business had failed.

## Factory Machinery

Often when women entered the world of technology, they were ignored. It was unbelievable that a woman could have anything to offer. This was the attitude that Margaret Knight (1838–1914) had to overcome to achieve

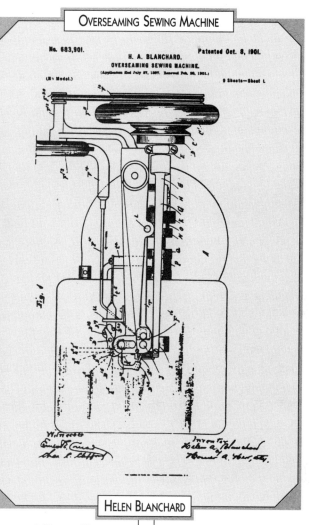

OVERSEAMING SEWING MACHINE

HELEN BLANCHARD

◆ Margaret Knight had to defend her rights as the inventor of the flat-bottomed paper bag machine in court. An argument against her was that a woman could not understand machinery.

her goals. Although she received twenty-six patents for devices used in industry, Knight had a hard time convincing men in the 1870s that she understood her own inventions.

Knight had a lifelong interest in technology. In her youth, she lived in Manchester, New Hampshire, where many cotton mills were located. Like many young girls in those times, she worked in a cotton mill when she was about ten years old. Even then, she showed her interest in machines by designing a device to make looms safer. Later she learned photography, engraving, and upholstery skills to support herself. She became interested in paper bags while working for the Columbia Paper Bag Company in Springfield, Massachusetts.

Before the 1870s, almost everything was packaged in wood, tin, or fabric. Customers carried their groceries in net bags, cardboard boxes, or even wooden boxes. Most of the paper bags that did exist were shaped like envelopes and could not hold much. The ones that had a flat bottom were made by hand. For years, men had been trying to design a machine that could make a bag with a flat bottom inexpensively. Unfortunately, the bag had to be folded and glued by hand, a tedious process.

Knight spent many months working out her ideas for a machine that would make a square-bottomed bag. She made numerous drawings, tried out the design on a wooden model, and finally had an iron model made to her specifications. But Charles F. Annan, a man who had seen her models, beat her to the Patent Office. She filed a lawsuit against him, claiming that he had copied her idea.

During the court battle, Annan and his lawyers tried to convince the court that Knight, being a woman, could not possibly have had enough knowledge of machinery to design such a machine. Fortunately, many people told the court that they had seen or been involved in the various phases of her work, from early discussions, writings, and drawings to the final machine. She won her case and received her patent in 1870.

On July 11, 1871, Knight received patent number 116,842 for an improvement to this machine. That document reads, "The nature of this invention consists in the peculiar construction of a machine for the manufacture of flat or satchel bottom bags from a continuous tube of paper fed from a roll over a form and cut, folded, pasted and delivered in the manner substantially as here-inafter described." The document goes on to describe in detail each part of the machine and how it works.

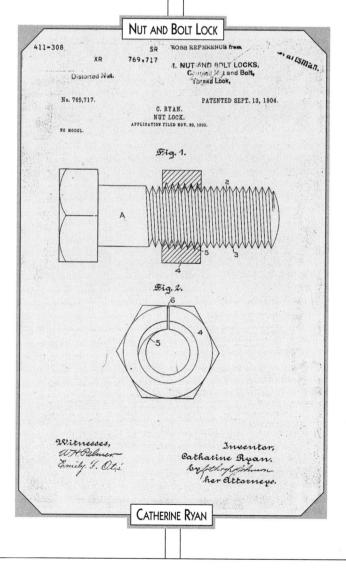

Knight and a Newton, Massachusetts, business-man set up the Eastern Paper Bag Company in Hartford, Connecticut, to profit from the machine. When she was invited to help install the machine in the factory where the bags were to be made, the workers would not listen to her advice, saying, "What does a woman know about machines?" Her answer was, in effect, "plenty."

Knight's later inventions included internal combustion engines, a resilient wheel, machinery for cutting shoe soles, and a window frame and sash.

## Transferring Knowledge

We often hear about a "woman's intuition." Of course, men have intuition as well. Inventors, whether they be men or women, often experience a "quick perception of truth without conscious attention or reasoning" — a dictionary definition

◆ Catherine Ryan, the inventor of the Nut and Bolt Lock shown on page 29.

*Inventors, whether they be men or women, often experience a "quick perception of truth without conscious attention or reasoning" — a dictionary definition of the word "intuition."*

of the word "intuition." Often this intuition is touched off by some ordinary, daily observation. Such was the case with Catherine Ryan (1865–1936). This housewife found a simple answer to a long-standing problem in the railroad industry.

During the 1800s, much money and energy went into keeping railroad tracks safe for operation. Frequent train and trolley accidents were caused by nuts that had loosened on the bolts that held the rails to the ties.

One day Ryan was strolling along a railroad track with her husband when she noticed railroad men tightening the bolts. That night, wondering about the problem, she noticed how her wedding ring was caught behind the joint of her finger. Instantly, she envisioned a locking nut. She took her idea to a machine shop, where the nut and bolt were made.

Ryan received a patent for the idea in 1904. The patent document gives this description: "In combination, a threaded bolt, the thread being cut deepest toward the ends of the threaded portion of the bolt, the entire outer edge of the thread being equidistant from the center of the bolt, and a split nut formed with an inner thread arranged to engage with said bolt-thread, the nut-thread being deeper than the shallowest portion of the bolt-thread.

"In combination, a threaded bolt and a split nut formed with a thread arranged to engage with said bolt-thread, said bolt thread being cut shallowest intermediate of its ends, and the thread of said nut being deeper than the shallowest portion of the bolt thread to cause spreading of said nut."

Ryan received six patents for various versions of her locking nut, the last in 1918. She lived to see her invention used on railroad and trolley tracks throughout the country.

## INVENTING FOR JUSTICE AND COMMON SENSE

After the Civil War, the number of people who argued, marched, and even went to jail for women's rights grew. These women and men, sometimes called feminists, encouraged women to become familiar with machinery and to put forward their creative ideas. Feminists organized exhibits of women's inventions at world's fairs and U.S. Centennial celebrations, and they wrote books and articles to call people's attention to women inventors. They disputed the idea that women could not understand mechanical and scientific concepts and therefore should not be allowed into schools of science or technology. They fought the idea that inventing was unwomanly.

Women who argued for the right to vote were called suffragettes, a word taken from the word "suffrage," meaning the right to vote. They included Matilda Gage, Susan B. Anthony, Elizabeth Cady Stanton, Lucy Stone, Amelia Bloomer, and many others. These advocates fought for and won, by the end of the nineteenth century, the right for every married woman in every state to own and control her own property, including her inventions. Why were *married* women specified? Because at the time, many states provided that when a woman married, her property became her husband's. Because a patent is legal property (like a home or a car), the husband also owned it.

Beginning in the eighteenth century, feminists fought against tight corsets and other impractical clothing customary at the time. Women who wore such impractical clothing frequently fainted and needing smelling salts. This gave the impression they were delicate. In many cases, it actually meant they needed to loosen their corsets so they could breathe. Pinched waists, bound bosoms, heavy petticoats, and long skirts made it impossible for women even to think of doing some kinds of work — or play. A woman had little choice of dress when she went out in public. She would disgrace her family if she wore trousers or a loose, comfortable dress that showed her ankles.

THE EMANCIPATION SUIT

The Emancipation Suit.

Patented August 3d, 1875.

The suit consists of the waist and drawers, either in one continuous garment, or made separate and buttoned together at the hips.

SUSAN TAYLOR CONVERSE

Women who hated their clothes were delighted when women's rights advocates began a reform movement to change women's clothing. In the 1870s, several women began designing garments that were light, fell freely from the shoulders, and did not get in the way when a woman walked upstairs or got into a buggy.

Susan Taylor Converse of Woburn, Massachusetts, devised a way to make cumbersome petticoats easier to manage and more comfortable. In 1875, she received a patent for an undergarment called the Emancipation Suit. It included pockets to free the breasts from compression, a series of buttons for attaching heavy petticoats and skirts, and long pants to keep the legs warm.

Converse received a twenty-five-cent royalty payment for each garment sold. That was a lot of money then. Some women's groups wanted her to lower the cost so that more women could afford to buy this wonderful new garment. She refused, saying that she "intended to use any invention for profit." In her mind, one of the most important rights for women was the right to earn a living.

## SUCCEEDING IN SPITE OF DOUBLE DISCRIMINATION

Although white women who entered the business world through their inventions encountered some prejudice, black women encountered even more. Yet many black women overcame much adversity to succeed in business. Two who stand out are Sarah Breedlove Walker and Marjorie Joyner, both of whom invented hair-care products. Both also promoted better education for black women while helping them achieve an appearance and style important to success in business and the professions. They created a new, extremely effective way of doing business that other companies have followed. The lives of these two women continue to inspire young people of all races.

### *Madam C.J. Walker*

Sarah Breedlove Walker was born on a plantation near Delta, Louisiana, in 1867, the child of former slaves. She picked cotton, became a washerwoman, and then became a cook. She married young and had a daughter, Lelia. Her maiden name was Breedlove.

By the time she was twenty, she was a widow, with full responsibility for herself and her child. She moved to St. Louis, Missouri, where she saw, in

some of the fine homes where she worked, an elegant way of life. Breedlove wanted that kind of life for herself and her child.

To reach this goal, Breedlove associated whenever possible with educated black men and women. A turning point in her life came when she heard a talk given by Margaret Murray Washington at a meeting of the National Association of Colored Women in St. Louis. (The speaker was the wife of the well-known black educator Booker T. Washington.) The theme was the rewards of hard work. Breedlove had always worked hard, but it seemed clear that she needed to find a different type of work if she were going to rise in society. More than that, she needed a new image. Her inventiveness in trying to change the way she looked led to a new life.

⬧ Sarah Breedlove Walker (driving the car above) told a gathering of the National Negro Business League in 1912, "I am a woman who came from the cotton fields of the South. I was promoted from there to the washtub. Then I was promoted to the cook kitchen, and from there I promoted myself into the business of manufacturing hair goods and preparations.... I have built my own factory on my own ground."

Breedlove had always thought that her hair was lifeless and hard to manage. After she moved to Denver, Colorado, to be near relatives, she found work in a drugstore. None of the products for sale seemed to improve her hair. She began experimenting with different mixtures of herbs and lotions until she created a lotion that made her hair glossy and healthy-looking. She began selling this lotion to other women, then hired women to sell it in the best black neighborhoods.

*Although white women who entered the business world through their inventions encountered some prejudice, black women encountered even more. Yet many black women overcame much adversity to succeed in business.*

In Denver, Breedlove married newspaperman Charles Walker. Together they created the Madam C.J. Walker Manufacturing Company in Indianapolis, Indiana. They sold Sarah Walker's own inventions: hair lotions, creams for black women, and an improved hairstyling hot comb. Walker continued to educate herself so that she was comfortable talking with people on all levels of society. She developed her own personal style and became known as the elegant and dignified "Madam Walker."

Walker's inventions, though never patented, helped her launch a business empire. She built a factory in Indianapolis to make her products and hired many more saleswomen. She traveled around the country setting up beauty salons where her products were used and sold. Women who worked in the salons were given special training and were called hair culturists. By 1918, Walker's company was earning $250,000 a year. Madam Walker had become the first American self-made woman millionaire.

Hairstyles change, and the products women want are replaced by new products. However, Walker's most important contribution to American business was not her products but the new system she created for marketing. She set up special schools around the country to teach black women how to care for their hair and skin and how to become teachers themselves. Of course, she also sold her own products. In addition, she developed a whole network of saleswomen who traveled door to door to introduce customers to the new products. These women then supervised others, who also sold the products. The door-to-door system and hairstyling lessons became the keys to her empire. Walker's methods have been adopted by many other businesses around the world.

In 1916, Walker let others take over the daily operation of her company and moved to New York. Her beautiful mansion on the Hudson River became a meeting place for poets, politicians, **entrepreneurs,** and her many friends. Although her health was poor, Walker continued to travel and champion the cause of civil rights for blacks and women. She died in 1919 at the age of fifty-one.

**ENTREPRENEUR**
A person who starts her or his own business.

### The "Grande Dame of Black Beauty Culture"

Born in 1896, Marjorie Stewart Joyner began working as a beautician for the Madam C.J. Walker Manufacturing Company when she arrived in Chicago as a young woman. Within a few years, her talent, imagination, and enthusiasm resulted in her being made national supervisor of the company's chain of beauty schools.

Joyner was never content to go along with things in the usual manner. She had a creative mind and enjoyed solving problems. She often used a curling iron to apply heat to hair and give it a set. Yet she heard women complain that their new hairdos did not stay "done" long enough. This was true both for black women who wanted to straighten and curl kinky hair and for white women with straight hair who wanted curls.

Joyner believed that she could invent a machine that would apply heat long enough to give a lasting set. She began experimenting with various devices. The result was one of the first electrically powered permanent wave machines. It included a dome that held curling irons, clamps, insulating sleeves, wires, and other mechanical devices. To quote her patent document, "The object of the invention is the construction of a simple and efficient machine that will wave the hair of both white and colored people."

Each strand of hair had to be carefully twisted and wrapped, then heated for the correct amount of time. This process could become uncomfortable. Joyner had a solution. She invented a "novel and efficient protector that is placed against the head of a person with a bunch of hair extending through, whereby the curling iron can be placed close to the head without any discomfort to the patron." The patents for the permanent wave machine and the scalp protector, issued in 1928 and 1929, became the property of her employer.

All her life, Joyner was a leader in the fight for the civil rights of minorities and women. By teaching and by example, she helped hundreds of black women achieve the confidence and skills they needed to get better

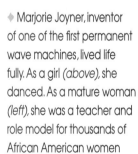

◆ Marjorie Joyner, inventor of one of the first permanent wave machines, lived life fully. As a girl (*above*), she danced. As a mature woman (*left*), she was a teacher and role model for thousands of African American women seeking better employment. In her nineties, she was a community leader.

jobs and command attention. She made beauty culture a respected vocation taught in many schools. When she was ninety-three, *The Washington Post* called her the "Grande Dame of Black Beauty Culture."

Joyner's influence went far beyond the beauty business. She helped the prominent educator Mary McLeod Bethune establish the National Council of Negro Women in 1935. By raising funds for Bethune-Cookman College in Daytona Beach, Florida, Joyner helped make possible higher education for many African Americans. During the 1940s, Joyner worked with First Lady Eleanor Roosevelt to help speed integration in American society.

For many years, Joyner was a beloved figure in Chicago, where she worked closely with the *Chicago Daily Defender* to promote African American history, culture, education, and social justice. Months before her death in 1994, she said, "I don't want to go to my grave with knowledge and not do something with it."

## A PIONEER IN WATER CONSERVATION

It has never been easy for people to change their views of what is right and wrong. For many in the nineteenth century and even later, it was simply not right for a woman to do men's work. When some women did, all kinds of odd arguments were used against them: Women's dresses were too wide for them to get through doors. Women were too emotional and frail. Some physicians claimed that women who exercised their brains too much were likely to become invalids. Inventor Harriet Strong showed that just the opposite was true.

Today the Colorado River basin in the American Southwest is one of the richest agricultural areas in the country. But one hundred years ago, farmers in the area were going broke trying to grow crops. Much of the change in this region is due to Strong's inventions and years of work to improve life through the use and control of water.

Born in 1844, Strong was raised on a ranch in California, one of six children. She attended a

◆ Harriet Strong's ideas for building dams in river canyons were not taken seriously until many years after she received patents for her designs. She was a leader in water conservation and the development of agriculture in the Southwest.

women's school for two years before marrying and raising four daughters. For seventeen years, she suffered from dizzy spells, back pains, and general weakness, staying in bed a good part of the time. Her husband, Charles, was a mining superintendent and frequently away on business.

The family moved often. At times, they could afford a nice home and servants. At other times, they had to scrimp to get by. During her years of ill health, Strong, often managing the household alone, also read and studied and continued to educate herself.

Disaster struck in 1883 when Charles committed suicide after a business failure. The shock of his death seriously affected Strong's health. In addition, the people to whom Charles had owed money were laying claim to her farm near Los Angeles. After several weeks, Strong got up out of bed, took charge of the family business, and apparently was never sick again.

For eight years, she fought for her property in the courts. In the end, she was able to save 220 acres for herself and her daughters. During that time, she was growing profitable crops such as walnuts, olives, oranges, and grapes. Her most successful crop was pampas grass. The large, graceful leaves of this plant were used for decorative purposes.

Strong also tried to make money on inventions — ideas that came out of the time when she was a sick housewife. Her first invention was a pole with a hook on the end that could be used to raise or lower windows in homes, schools, and churches or for hanging garments in tall closets. She received a patent for it and sold it as the Bedford Window Attachment. Strong also received patents for an improved hook-and-eye fastener and an improved window-sash holder. She made little profit from these inventions, but she was learning lessons about business that she would use later in other projects.

Strong's ranch and those of other farmers were not as productive as they might have been because there was not enough water for their crops. When the rains came, the rivers and streams filled irrigation ditches with water. But the rest of the time, the land was dry. Strong proposed building a series of dams in river canyons to create reservoirs of water. Engineers found the idea amazing and impossible, even though she was

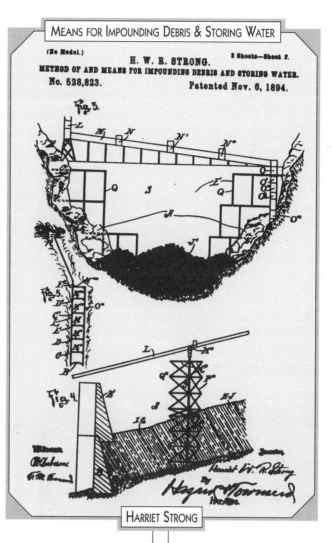

HARRIET STRONG

◆ This "means for impounding debris and storing water" was one of Strong's visionary ideas for bringing water to crops in the Southwest.

granted a patent for the design in 1887.

Strong did not let others' lack of faith hold her back. In 1894, she received a patent for a method of gathering and holding rock, gravel, and other coarse, heavy material carried by rivers and using it to strengthen dams. Meanwhile, she was always trying new crops and new ways of growing things. She was often successful and became well-known for her ideas in agriculture and for promoting water conservation.

In time, her inventions earned her two awards at the World's Columbian Exposition in Chicago in 1893. This event brought together ideas for new technology in many different industries. To explain her water conservation concepts, she constructed a small working model of a series of dams, which she used to irrigate a miniature orange grove. For this, she won a medal for practical ideas in the field of agriculture. The Department of Mining also gave her a medal for her device for collecting debris and storing water.

Strong became active in civic matters, speaking out for women's rights. She became the first woman on the Los Angeles Chamber of Commerce. A major problem for the area was flooding, as heavy rains regularly destroyed buildings and crops. Strong organized landowners to help develop plans to channel the rainwater and build reservoirs to contain it. She guided the planning process, which involved endless meetings, debates, and consultations with politicians, engineers, and civic leaders. In 1915, the Los Angeles County Flood Control Act was passed to provide state tax money for a huge water conservation project. This was the greatest engineering project of southern California to date.

In 1918, Strong testified before Congress on the need for water conservation in the Southwest. She presented her plan for a series of dams in part of the Grand Canyon. It would create more parkland, produce electric power, and allow the agricultural development of the entire Southwest. She freely offered the use of her ideas for the benefit of the country. Years later, the Colorado River Project was undertaken. This project has transformed the nature of agriculture in the Southwest and permitted the development of a great urban center.

## MEETING THE CHALLENGES OF WORLD WAR

During World Wars I and II, women pitched in to replace the men who were called away from factories, laboratories, hospitals, and other businesses. Through

♦ During World War II, thousands of American women helped make weapons and other defense-related machinery. The women shown here are working on the noses of fighter planes at Douglas Aircraft's Long Beach, California, plant around 1943.

inventions, they also helped the war effort in many ways.

A 1923 report from the U.S. Department of Labor lists these inventions by women: Automatic Pistol; Bomb-Launching Apparatus; Cane-Gun; Rear Sight for Guns; Mine; Percussion and Ignition Fuse; Railway Torpedo; Single Trigger Mechanism Submarine; Torpedo Guard. Women invented many other defense-related devices during the Second World War.

In 1945, Henrietta Bradberry, an African American woman from Chicago, was granted a patent for her device for discharging torpedoes underwater. She described it as "practical in its construction, efficient and useful in its operation and of such simple construction that it can be produced economically in quantity production." Marguerite Shue-wen Chang's name appears on at least eight patents relating to defense, including one for a device that triggered an underground nuclear explosive in a 1969 Atomic Energy Commission test.

### The Dummy Solution

At the start of World War II, the U.S. Navy designed huge rubber fuel tanks for planes and submarines. They were made by gluing and **vulcanizing** sheets of rubber over a wooden form, or mold. But the Navy had not figured out how to remove the mold.

Engineers at U.S. Rubber, the company making the tanks for the Navy, thought specially treated paper might be the solution. They asked Lillian Greneker, a New York inventor and businesswoman known for her expertise with paper, for advice. She headed the Greneker Corporation, a paper manufacturing company in Pleasantville, New York.

Greneker insisted that plaster, not paper, was the answer. The engineers, who had already experimented with plaster, said that it would not work. Greneker decided to try her idea in her own shop with the help of a plaster-birdbath maker. She had what she needed at hand: mannequins, or store dummies, used for modeling clothing, and her own patented methods for creating these flexible mannequins out of cellophane or laminated (glued) paper.

**VULCANIZE**
A way of chemically changing rubber so that it is strong and elastic.

◆ Lillian Greneker used what she learned in creating mannequins for store windows to create a form for fuel tanks used in World War II.

As an experiment, Greneker and her assistant poured plaster into a hollow mannequin's leg. They also dropped a rope into the leg so that it would be embedded in the plaster when the plaster hardened. The rope extended from the top of the leg. When it was pulled, the plaster broke into pieces and could be removed.

Greneker went back to U.S. Rubber and demonstrated her idea. She suggested that they make plaster molds of the tanks in two halves and join them together. Workers could stretch vulcanized rubber sheeting over each mold. When the rubber had hardened, they could yank the rope. The plaster would break into pieces and could be removed through a small opening in the rubber tank.

"It's too easy!" they said. "Only a woman would come up with an idea like that." However, the company's chief engineers agreed to give it a try. It worked beautifully. As a result, Greneker's company helped manufacture

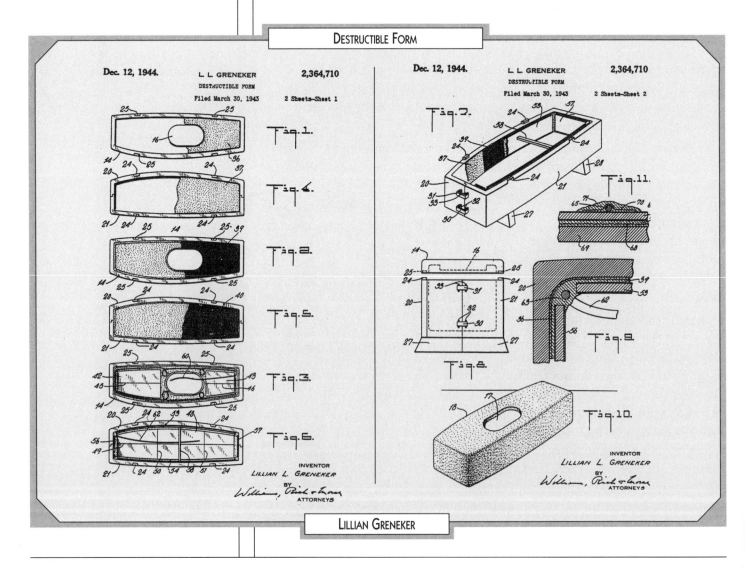

DESTRUCTIBLE FORM

LILLIAN GRENEKER

the fuel tanks so badly needed for the Grumman Hellcat fighter plane. They cranked out five tanks a day while the military provided maximum security.

Greneker received fifteen patents between 1937 and 1945, including three for destructible forms, indicating that she kept improving her design. One of these patents, dated March 30, 1943, reads, "This invention relates to a destructible form which is particularly useful in the manufacture of fuel tanks and cells or articles made of rubber or other material. It is not concerned with the particular shape of the form, but merely with its construction, since of course the construction may be used in forms having an infinite variety of shapes and sizes."

Another of her inventions was a device called Fingertips, by which small tools could be attached to a person's fingers. For instance, artists could attach five different brushes to their fingers and paint much more quickly, without ever having to lay one brush down to pick up another. Fingertips did not catch on with the public, but Greneker never gave up on it. When she was eighty-five, she received a patent for a new version of the device. There is no record of its ever being sold.

### Open Doors

An important and lasting effect of the two world wars was that women were able to break into new fields. Highly trained women who had not been able to find jobs before were taken on in factories, research laboratories, and other businesses.

In the 1960s, the revitalized women's movement began changing ideas concerning women's role in society. After a long struggle, women have finally gained acceptance in most institutions of higher learning. Some women may still be denied jobs because of their gender, but for the most part, it is against the law for employers to discriminate against women. Today women work in nearly every profession and trade. The challenge for young women is to take advantage of opportunities and prepare themselves for whatever career they wish to pursue.

Since the 1960s, the number of women applying for patents has increased every year. During the 1950s, about one and a half percent of patents were in a woman's name, not a great leap forward from 1900. By 1993, the number of patents issued to women had risen to about eight percent of all those issued. Women inventors are finally starting to make a name for themselves in much greater numbers.

> *Women have finally gained acceptance in most institutions of higher learning. The challenge for young women is to take advantage of opportunities and prepare themselves for whatever career they wish to pursue.*

# ACTIVITIES

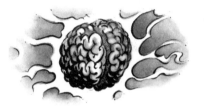

## *Project 1*

## FORCED RELATIONS

### Objective

This exercise in creativity asks students to think of new ways to use ordinary objects. The time limitations and restriction to a particular place help to focus the activity and provide the fun of seeing how different students come up with different inventions using similar objects.

Putting things together in a new way forces you to see things differently. Actually placing things side by side and positioning or connecting them in unusual ways may give you some ideas.

**1. Here and now I am aware of ...** Go to your kitchen with paper, pencil, and timer. For fifteen minutes, list everything that you cannot eat (countertop, stove, light fixture, fork, and so on).

**2. Combine to invent.** From the list, combine two, three, or more items to create an improvement. Don't judge too soon. Feel free to list some bizarre ideas; you can tone them down later to be more practical. Can you list thirty new inventions? More?

**3. Implement.** Draw your invention. Describe it. Create a patent application like the sample shown at the end of Appendix 1. Submit your application to a "patent examiner" (your teacher) to see whether a patent will be granted.

## *Project 2*

## A DAY IN 1870

### Objective

Students gain experience in using library facilities, see an inventor in the context of her historical period, and gain knowledge of the different tasks involved in creating a newspaper. This is a cooperative learning activity.

As a class, create a newspaper front page for one day in the year 1870. Decide on where in the United States the paper is published. Select one person to be editor-in-chief, another to be assistant editor. Decide who will be reporters (several), headline writers (two), copy editors (one or two) to check spelling and grammar, illustrators (one or two), and the layout artist (to design the page).

**1.** The editor-in-chief assigns one reporter to research and write a story about Margaret Knight. (Read "Factory Machinery." You can find out more about her in the book *Feminine Ingenuity* by Anne L. Macdonald, which is listed in the bibliography.)

**2.** The editors and reporters do library research to find out some things that happened between 1865 and 1875 in the area where the paper is published and elsewhere in the United States and the world. This material will be reported in the paper as if it happened on one day.

**3.** Each reporter selects one event that she or he considers important or historical. Also, each reporter writes down or makes copies of articles about three not-so-important local events. The reporters should try to come up with different events. They should write only as many words as might appear in one column before the article is continued on another page.

**4.** The editor-in-chief and assistant editor look over all the articles presented by the reporters and choose the ones they want for the front page. They should choose one major story, several less important stories, and the Margaret Knight story.

**5.** The headline writers create snappy headlines.

**6.** The copy editors make the necessary corrections.

**7.** The illustrators find and photocopy pictures to illustrate the articles, or they may draw them.

**8.** The editors make sure they have everything that they need for the front page.

**9.** The layout artist arranges all this material and discusses with the editor-in-chief what should be cut.

**10.** The layout artist "pastes up" the front page, then asks the editors and copy editors to check it over.

Corrections are made, the editor photocopies the page, and the assistant editor distributes it to the class.

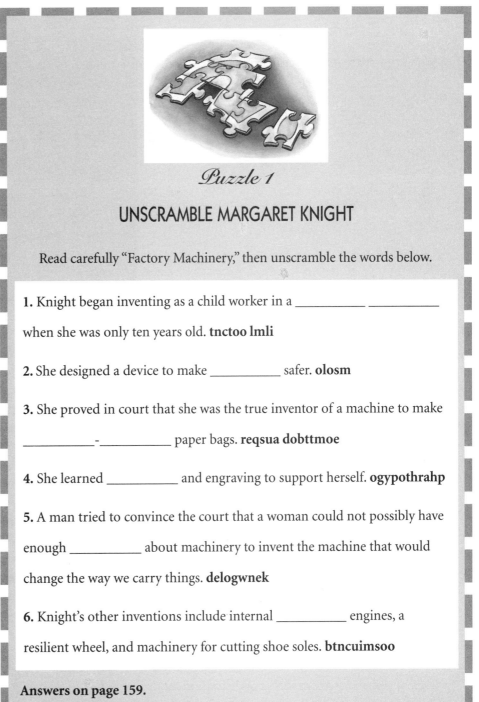

*Puzzle 1*

## UNSCRAMBLE MARGARET KNIGHT

Read carefully "Factory Machinery," then unscramble the words below.

**1.** Knight began inventing as a child worker in a _____ _____ when she was only ten years old. **tnctoo lmli**

**2.** She designed a device to make _____ safer. **olosm**

**3.** She proved in court that she was the true inventor of a machine to make _____-_____ paper bags. **reqsua dobttmoe**

**4.** She learned _____ and engraving to support herself. **ogypothrahp**

**5.** A man tried to convince the court that a woman could not possibly have enough _____ about machinery to invent the machine that would change the way we carry things. **delogwnek**

**6.** Knight's other inventions include internal _____ engines, a resilient wheel, and machinery for cutting shoe soles. **btncuimsoo**

**Answers on page 159.**

*Puzzle 2*

## MATCH THE PROBLEM WITH THE SOLUTION

The statements in the box below express problems. Those beneath the box tell how inventors you read about in this chapter solved the problems. Write the letter of the solution on the line beside the number of the matching problem.

____ **1.** We have no idea what the enemy is up to, especially at sea.

____ **2.** Isn't there some way I can keep my hands from getting burned on the handle of an iron?

____ **3.** This soldier is badly wounded, but if we move him, we will make the injury worse.

____ **4.** It's taking much too long to make these garments.

____ **5.** I could do many jobs if my clothes didn't make it impossible.

____ **6.** Riding on a train can be a high-risk activity.

____ **7.** I can't do a thing with my hair.

____ **8.** How can we get the mold out of the rubber fuel tank?

**a.** Madam C.J. Walker created her own hair lotions.

**b.** Catherine Ryan invented self-locking nuts and bolts to secure railroad tracks to ties.

**c.** Susan Converse designed an entirely new kind of undergarment for women.

**d.** With Clarissa Britain's device, a wounded man could be taken to a hospital without being lifted off the stretcher.

**e.** Lillian Greneker put a rope inside a plaster mold, and when the rubber tank had hardened, she pulled on the rope. The plaster broke, and the pieces could be removed through a small opening in the tank.

**f.** Sarah Mather designed an underwater telescope for "locating and studying underwater objects."

**g.** Helen Blanchard's new sewing machine sewed and trimmed knitted fabrics in one operation.

**h.** One of Mary Potts's inventions was a set of three irons with one removable handle. The ironer could always have a hot iron and a cool handle.

Answers on page 159.

*Think About It*

**Objective**

Students gain perspective about their world by comparing conditions of the past with those of the present.

**1.** In the past, women's clothing kept them from participating in many activities. Do any current customs having to do with dress and appearance affect what women can do? Do any affect what men can do?

**2.** Margaret Knight invented machinery to mass-produce square-bottomed paper bags. What inventions of the past fifty years have made an important difference in how things are carried? Will paper bags become obsolete?

**3.** When Mary Potts invented a new kind of iron, it made a big difference in the lives of girls and women. Why? Do new and better irons mean as much to women today as they did in the nineteenth century? Why? How many products can you think of that make it easier to keep clothes looking neat?

**4.** Elias Howe is famous for inventing the sewing machine. Why is Helen Blanchard, who received more than twenty patents for sewing machine inventions, not equally famous? Why is knowledge of prior technology important to an inventor? Why is it important to patent each improvement? (You can find a discussion of the patent process in Appendix 1.)

**5.** Many people invent wonderful devices but never become famous or rich. Madam C.J. Walker was an exception. What did she do with the lotion she originally made for herself? It has been said that her most important "invention" was her method of selling. Many other companies have followed her example. What did she do that was so significant? How were similar products sold before?

**6.** Lillian Greneker was an expert in making paper products. She was an inventor of store mannequins (models of the human form) made of plaster or shredded paper mixed with glue to form a molding material (papier-mâché) in the late 1930s and early 1940s. Why did the U.S. Navy think that her expertise could help them in making rubber fuel tanks to be used in planes and submarines? What qualities do paper and plaster have? How do these materials compare with wood, stone, and metal? When is paper or plaster superior to wood, stone, or metal?

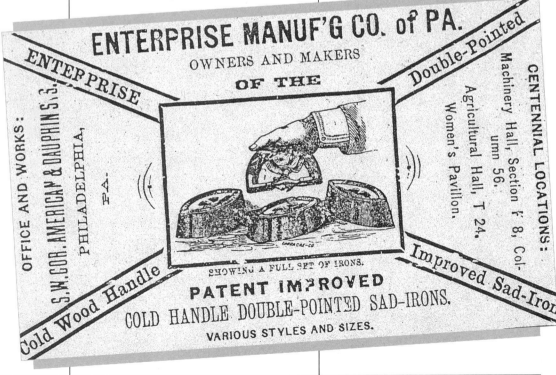

## The Way You See It

### Objective
Suggestions for writing assignments. To encourage students to think independently about events in history and how they relate to today. To encourage students to do outside reading.

**1.** Read other books or articles about Sarah Breedlove Walker and explain what you think are the most interesting facts about her life.

**2.** In the past, learning how to control rivers in the American Southwest was of great importance to agriculture. Today many people want water for many uses. What are some of these uses? What dangers do they pose for the water supply? What are conservationists trying to do to solve these problems? How might new technology help?

**3.** Since before the Civil War, women have been fighting for equal rights. What were some of their early victories? Some names associated with the struggle during the nineteenth century are Julia Ward Howe, Lucretia Mott, Elizabeth Cady Stanton, Susan B. Anthony, and Lucy Stone.

☞ Research one or more of these women or other well-known women of the time who were active in the women's rights movement. What were the main rights they wanted and the methods they used to try to obtain them? Why were some of these women called "radical"?

☞ Do you know of any women in the women's rights movement today who might be called "radical"? If so, why?

## Imagine That!

### Objective
To learn by doing, with cross-curriculum application. Preparation includes reading and discussing the chapter sections about the inventors or inventions mentioned.

**1. Shake it up!** The Shakers, a religious group in early America, held themselves apart from the world, inventing most of the things they needed. Although the record is unclear, a Shaker woman is said to have invented the circular saw. See if you can find mention of this in any reference material in the library. Look in books about tools and about Shakers. Find out what other useful things Shakers invented. (If possible, find a copy of the April 1983 issue of *COBBLE-STONE* magazine on the Shakers.)

**2. Art activity.** Make a colorful poster about women inventors. Use as few or as many as you want to make an interesting display. You can make a collage or group together several pictures for a special effect. Use photographs of the women and pictures of their inventions if they are available. Or draw your own pictures. You might create a symbol for the person or her invention. For instance, Harriet Strong's ideas for water control and conservation led to growing crops in formerly dry, barren regions. How could you symbolize this?

**3. An individual or small group project.** When people speak of "Rosie the Riveter," whom do they mean? Ask women or men who were young adults during the 1940s. Interview some of the women to find out what they were doing during the war. Try to find at least three women who took a wartime job that was available to them only because so many men were serving in the armed forces. If you find a woman with an interesting story, arrange, if possible, to audiotape or videotape (with sound) her as she tells her own story. Ask if she has pictures from that era or other objects that would be of interest in a video.

**4. Action!** Review the sections in

this chapter about the following inventors: Margaret Knight, Madam C.J. Walker, Marjorie Joyner, Harriet Strong, Lillian Greneker. Have three to five students prepare to act out, in pantomime, three incidents in the life of one of these women. If the other students cannot identify the woman after the first incident is acted out, the second may be acted out and then the third.

**5. Cartooning.** Create a series of cartoons about the life of Harriet Strong. Read "A Pioneer in Water Conservation" to find incidents that you can illustrate. (One might show her lying sick in bed, raising a window with the device she invented.) Include as many panels as needed. Use color if you like.

Put a few words above or on each picture describing what is happening. Imagine what the person in the picture might be thinking. The words can be those of a narrator, or someone telling the story. Or they might be the words of the person in the picture.

**6. The history of language.** When we use a special tool to smooth clothing, we call the process "ironing." These words come from iron, the material used to make the tool. Sometimes we refer to the process of smoothing clothes as "pressing." Can you guess why? Early irons did not work very well, and the people using them had to press very hard. That also is how the printing press got its name.

☞ Can you identify the history of other words? Make a list of words you find interesting and, using a special dictionary concerned with word origins, look up their meaning. Then create riddles based on these words.

☞ For example, the word "pinafore" today refers to a kind of apron usually worn by girls or women over a dress. If you look up its origin, you will find that its meaning goes back to the custom of printers pinning an apron over the front of their shirts to protect their clothing from ink stains. Here is one way to use this information in a riddle:

**"A**

**_ _ _ _ _ _ _ _**
**[pinafore]**
**is an apron that does not tie around the neck. Printers would**

**_ _ _**
**[pin]**
**it to their shirts or blouses."**

When you get a good collection of riddles, try them out on your parents and teachers. See if they can fill in the right words.

*You Say Yes; I Say No*

**Objective**
Topics for debate.

1. Women should show their interest in peace and harmony in the world by inventing ways to help the environment. They should leave the invention of weapons to men. Do you agree or disagree?

2. If girls and boys were separated in science classes, girls would do better than they do in mixed-gender classes. Do you agree or disagree?

# Chapter

## 3

# INVENTING TO

**GENE**
A tiny unit in an animal or a plant that contains the directions for how the animal or plant will grow.

IN THE PAST, THE WORD "INVENTION" BROUGHT TO MIND items like Benjamin Franklin's stove — things you could see and get your hands on. Now inventions often involve things we cannot see and can barely imagine. For example, women and men can now change plants by adding **genes.**

In addition, most inventing is now done not by one individual, but by men and women working together as a research team for a large institution. The number of women researchers is still small compared to the number of men, but women are playing important roles in the development of extraordinary new products and technologies.

Several of the women inventors in this chapter entered the world of scientific research before the doors were opened to women in general. Their exceptional talents and the scarcity of men in research laboratories during World War II often won them entrance. Their achievements have helped make the path to invention much easier for women today.

## PIONEERS IN COMPUTER TECHNOLOGY

Computers have changed the way people do almost everything — and certainly the way people solve problems and invent. Computer technology is changing so fast that anything considered state-of-the-art today will be out-of-date tomorrow. Women are on the cutting edge of this development.

### The First User-Friendly Computers

Among the early pioneers in the use of computers was Grace Murray Hopper (1906–1992). She is considered the "mother"

◆ The commanding officer of the USS *Constitution* presents Grace Hopper with a bouquet of flowers after she received the Distinguished Service Medal.

# CHANGE OUR LIVES

of the U.S. Navy's computerized data automation system (a system of storing information in computers) and was known as "Amazing Grace."

Born Grace Murray, she was the first woman to graduate from Yale University with a Ph.D. in math. After graduation, she became a professor of mathematics at Vassar College. For several years, she was married to Vincent Hopper, a university professor. When the United States entered World War II, she joined the U.S. Naval Reserve with the rank of midshipman. Later she was called to active duty to work with computers, which were important to the war effort. Hopper became one of the first three programmers to work on the first large digital computer, the Mark I.

In the early 1940s, computers were mainly huge calculating machines. Hopper came up with the concept of feeding a computer human-oriented instructions — words like "stop" and "execute" — and letting it translate them into its own computer language.

"Everyone said I could not," a *New York Times* article reported her as saying, "so we went ahead and did it." The result was the computer language COBOL (Common Business-Oriented Language). As a result, nonmathematicians were able for the first time to use computers for all kinds of tasks in business and daily life. COBOL is the most widely used computer business language in the world. (For a discussion of COBOL and more about Hopper, see *Grace Hopper: Navy Admiral and Computer Pioneer* by Charlene W. Billings, which is listed in the bibliography.)

Hopper was promoted to lieutenant in 1944 and rose to the rank of lieu-

♦ Captain Grace M. Hopper at her desk in Washington, D.C., when she was head of the Navy Programming Section of the Office of the Chief of Naval Operations in 1976. She was the first Naval Reserve woman to be called back to active duty.

tenant commander in 1957. The Navy transferred her to Reserve status in January 1967, then brought her back to active duty in August to help standardize the various computer languages that had been created over the years so that different computers could "talk" to each other. One of her major accomplishments during the next few years was the development of the Navy's Early Automatic Coding System. Hopper rose to the rank of captain in 1973 and commodore in 1983. In 1985, she achieved the rank of rear admiral, becoming the first woman admiral in the Navy.

In her later years, Hopper emphasized that we do not need bigger computers that can do many things, but systems of computers that can operate at the same time and talk to each other. For instance, she envisioned computers specially designed for tracking waves at the bottom of the ocean, for weather forecasting, and for control of scarce water resources.

Hopper encouraged inventiveness in others. To prove that things do not always have to be done the same way, she put a clock in her office with the numbers running backward.

Hopper believed in taking risks. "It's harder to get permission than to apologize later," she told young people. "Just do it!" She liked to make ideas as concrete as possible. She used to show her audiences a one-and-a-half-inch-long piece of wire and say, "This is the distance a piece of information can travel in a computer in a nanosecond [a billionth of a second]."

Hopper made her **software** innovations before software came under patent protection. But she is widely recognized as an inventor, and many patented inventions of later software developers owe much to her ground-breaking work. In 1984, she was inducted into the Engineering and Science Hall of Fame. This was a great honor, as only six others had been so honored. Among them were Jonas Salk, for his polio vaccine; R. Buckminster Fuller, famous for the geodesic dome; and Thomas Edison, known for many inventions, including the electric light bulb. Honored at the same time as Hopper were George Washington Carver for his innovations in agriculture and Henry Heimlich, who had devised the Heimlich maneuver, which has saved thousands of people from choking.

The citation for Hopper states, "In tribute to your superior technical competence and mathematical genius; in tribute to your creative leadership, vision and commitment as a computer pioneer; in tribute to your setting a foremost example as an author and inventor; in tribute to your dedication to the human and humane elements of teaching, learning and scholarship; and in tribute to your insights and innovations in meeting the challenges of rapidly changing times, we induct you — Commodore Grace Murray Hopper — into the Engineering and Science Hall of Fame."

## Controlling Telephone Calls

Computer engineer Erna Schneider Hoover drafted an essential part of the design of the country's first electronic telephone switching system while in a hospital bed following the birth of her second daughter.

Hoover went to work for Bell Laboratories in New Jersey in 1954. Her background was very unusual for a woman: She had a Ph.D. in the philosophy and foundations of mathematics from Yale University. She arrived at Bell Labs during a time of change. "I grew up with computers, in the sense that my career began just at the time that computers were becoming important in industry," she says. Hoover used her skills in mathematics to help develop new computer **hardware** and software systems, including the Electronic Switching System widely used today for connecting people by telephone.

One of the problems in the early 1970s was computer overload when many people were trying to make telephone calls at the same time. Hoover and her associate Barry J. Eckhart developed software called the Feedback Control Monitor for Stored Program Data Processing System. This software provided a way of regulating the number of calls accepted and per-

**SOFTWARE**
The instructions and information given to a computer. For instance, a computer game is software that tells the computer what to display on the TV or video screen. The game's software also tells the computer what to do when the player "talks" to the computer by moving the joystick or typing in her or his name using the keyboard.

**HARDWARE**
The mechanical, magnetic, and electronic design structure and devices of a computer.

♦ Computer engineer Erna S. Hoover devised a way to overcome a problem of computer overload while working for Bell Laboratories in 1971. As a result, we are all easily connected by telephone.

mitting the largest possible number to be completed. The software was patented in 1971.

As a result of her work on the patent and her overall contributions, Hoover became the first woman to head a technical department for Bell Labs. She helped develop more complex computer programs that are used in keeping out-of-doors telephone equipment in service.

Born in Irvington, New Jersey, in 1926, Hoover grew up in South Orange, the daughter of a dentist and a former schoolteacher. "In school I hated having to add up numbers, but I enjoyed solving problems in algebra and geometry," she says. As a young woman, she had a wide range of interests, including medieval and classical history, logic, and philosophy. She majored in these subjects at Wellesley College, in Massachusetts, from which she graduated in 1948.

After receiving her Ph.D., Hoover taught philosophy, especially logic and the philosophy of science, at Swarthmore College. She married a physicist who had accepted a job at Bell Labs in northern New Jersey. "Having been promoted to the rank of assistant professor, I had a hard time finding another comparable job in the New Jersey–New York area because of prejudice against women," she says. Because symbolic logic is used to describe the behavior of electric and electronic circuits used in computers, she finally landed a job at Bell Labs.

Hoover retired from Bell Labs in 1983. Since then, she has worked to improve education in New Jersey on all levels, with a special concern for the sciences. In April 1994, she helped organize a conference in Montclair, New Jersey, aimed at encouraging girls to study math and science. The conference, sponsored by the American Association of University Women and the Girl Scouts of America, was called "Expanding Your Horizons." It brought two hundred preteen girls together with women from a variety of fields. Among the women were veterinarians, building contractors, pilots and flight instructors, graphic designers, and dietitians. Using hands-on activities, they showed the girls how math and science help them in their work.

Hoover also visits schools to talk to students about the importance and rewards of studying science. From 1977 to 1989, she served on the board of trustees at Trenton State College, helping it to receive recognition as one of the outstanding comprehensive colleges in the United States. She also has served on the Board of Higher Education for the State of New Jersey.

Today inventors in all areas of science and technology use computers in various phases of the invention process. Any new software can be copyrighted as an original written work. However, to receive a patent, a software program must have a specific application, or use. It must relate directly to a process, a machine, an article of manufacture, or a chemical composition. Hoover's patent for Bell Labs, for instance, was designed for the specific function of controlling telephone calls.

## CHEMISTS LEAD THE FIELD

Our lives have been changed through chemistry, and women have been especially important in this field. A study of patents granted between 1977 and 1988 shows that women inventors were more active in chemical technologies than in any other field. More than four hundred patents granted for chemical technologies during this twelve-year period included women's names, and many more have since been added to the list. Products range from new medicines to new building materials.

*Hoover used her skills in mathematics to help develop new computer hardware and software systems, including the Electronic Switching System widely used today for connecting people by telephone.*

*Katharine Blodgett*

Katharine Blodgett (1898–1979) was one of the first women to make a name for herself as a scientist and an inventor. She invented "invisible glass," a nonglare glass used in products ranging from telescopes and cameras to picture frames.

Blodgett was born and raised in Schenectady, New York. Her father, a patent attorney for General Electric, died before she was born. Her excellent grades in high school earned her a scholarship to Bryn Mawr College, in Pennsylvania, where she became interested in physics.

Although it was unusual for a woman at that time to go on to higher education in science, Blodgett was encouraged to do so. Her most important supporter was Irving Langmuir, a research scientist at G.E. and a Nobel Prize winner in chemistry. With recommendations from Langmuir and others, Blodgett was accepted as a graduate student at the University of Chicago, from which she received a master of science degree in 1918.

Blodgett was the first woman to be hired as a research scientist by the

**MOLECULE**
Two or more atoms held together in a definite arrangement by electrical forces. The smallest subdivision of a compound.

G.E. Research Laboratory in Schenectady. She worked in surface chemistry, the study of the chemical and physical properties of the surface of objects. Six years later, she left G.E. to continue her scientific training at Cambridge University in England. In 1926, she became the first woman to receive a Ph.D. in physics from the university. After receiving her degree, she returned to G.E.

When Blodgett began working at G.E., it was known that oily substances form a layer on water that is only one **molecule** thick. G.E. researchers were interested in this fact. They thought it could lead to new discoveries that might be useful in creating new technologies. The question that concerned Blodgett was "How can you measure something that is only a few millionths of an inch thick?" She discovered a way to do this using a technique based on her knowledge of light, color, and chemistry.

After many laboratory experiments, Blodgett was successful in applying layers of sodium stearate (a kind of soap) to a glass plate. Each time she lowered a plate of glass into the soap solution, a film only one molecule thick stayed on the plate when it was removed. Each time a layer was added to the plate, the film reflected a different color in the presence of white light. By noting the color of the film, Blodgett could tell how many molecules thick it was. G.E. patented her method of applying monomolecular (single-molecule) layers of film to a surface in 1933.

This and other experiments she conducted over the next few years resulted in the development of what G.E. called a nonreflecting invisible glass, patented in 1938. Ordinary glass is visible because of the light rays reflected from its surface. When a film is placed on the glass, there is a reflection from the film as well as from the glass. Blodgett discovered that a film of forty-four layers of transparent liquid soap, about four-millionths of an inch thick, made sheets of glass invisible. Many later advances in this technology have been based on her work.

During World War II, Blodgett researched ways to use the thin film she had invented to help with information gathering and to save lives. As a result, periscopes and aerial cameras were coated with the film to increase their efficiency. Aircraft wings were deiced faster due to a coating of the film. And Allied troops were given critical cover during invasions of enemy-held territory with the help of smoke screens that included the film.

Irving Langmuir, with whom Blodgett wrote many scientific papers, described her as "a gifted experimenter" with a "rare combination of theoretical and practical ability." She was honored by many colleges and universities and received the 1942 Annual Achievement Award from the American Association of University Women for her work in surface chemistry.

## Ruth Benerito

Cotton is a wonderful fabric — but one that has resulted in hours of ironing. Ruth Benerito helped to change all that. Through numerous experiments with cotton molecules, observing reactions under various controlled conditions, she found a way to cover cotton with a transparent film that makes it wrinkle resistant.

Benerito has done her research as a scientist for the U.S. Department of Agriculture (USDA). She is the author or coauthor

*"I like chemistry because I can keep thinking of smaller and smaller things,"* Ruth Benerito once said. *"It is fun! I prefer it to thinking about the whole universe — that, to me, is mind-boggling!"*

of fifty-one patents resulting from thirty-three years of service at the Southern Regional Research Center in New Orleans, Louisiana. Many of her patents (owned by the USDA) deal with fabrics, but not all of them do. One of the most important is for a nutritious solution for people who cannot eat and must be fed a liquid through their veins. This **intravenous fatty emulsion** provides more **calories** to patients and was created in time to help many of those wounded during the Korean War (1950–1953).

In 1979, Benerito received the highest award given by the USDA for her distinguished service and contributions as a teacher and researcher. Ironically, in 1936, when she had just graduated from college with a bachelor of science degree, no one would hire her as a science teacher because she was a woman. For a while, the only job she could get in her field was as a laboratory technician in a New Orleans hospital — for no pay! Eventually, she landed a teaching position at Tulane University, but when the university refused to promote her, she decided to stay on at her summer job at a nearby USDA laboratory. A lifetime of research, inventing, and teaching at all levels resulted from this decision.

**INTRAVENOUS FATTY EMULSION**
Intravenous means "through the veins." Often sick people who cannot eat are fed this way. Usually a long, narrow tube carries the special liquid food from a bag to a needle inserted in one of the patient's veins. A fatty emulsion is a liquid containing invisible fatty particles that absorb other substances. These particles help the body absorb more nutrients and provide a higher calorie intake (more energy).

**CALORIE**
A measurement of energy provided by food.

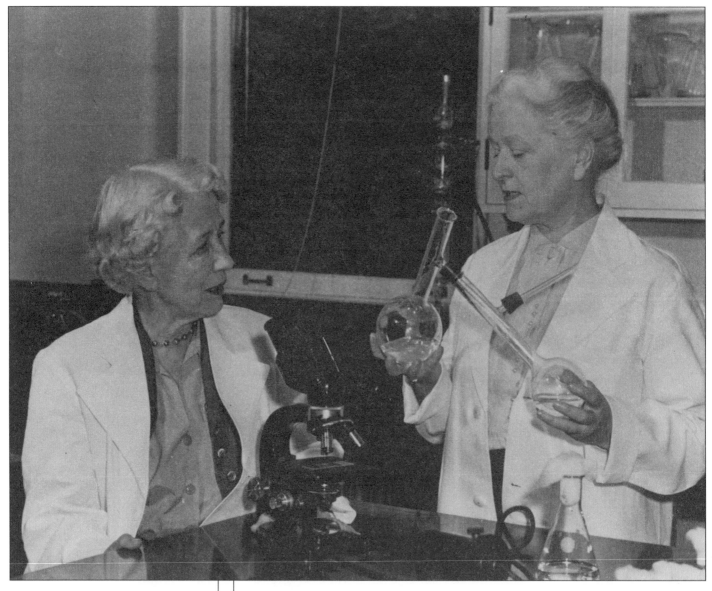

♦ Chemist Rachel Brown (right) and microbiologist Elizabeth Hazen (left) made a major medical breakthrough in 1957 by developing the drug nystatin — the first successful antiobiotic for treating fungal infections. In April 1994, years after both had died, they became the second and third women inducted into the National Inventors Hall of Fame.

## *Rachel Fuller Brown and Elizabeth Lee Hazen*

Sometimes an inventor can get help with the process of applying for a patent and marketing an invention. In some cases, the inventor will choose to give up any profits so that an invention can reach the public more quickly. This was true for chemist Rachel Fuller Brown and microbiologist Elizabeth Lee Hazen of the New York State Department of Health in 1957. They worked together for several years to find a cure for fungal infections.

Fungi are unicell (one-celled) organisms that feed on dead or living organic matter. During World War II, many men contracted fungal infections while fighting in jungles. A treatment for these and other fungal infections of the skin, mouth, throat, vagina, and intestinal tract was needed.

Hazen and Brown looked at soil samples from all over the world, searching for a bacterium that could destroy fungi. They finally found what they were looking for in a soil sample taken from a farm in Virginia. They used this bacterium to create a medicine that they named nystatin, in honor of the New York State laboratory where they worked.

Nystatin was a major medical breakthrough because it kills the fungus without harming the essential bacteria in the body that control fungi. In other words, it does not have any bad side effects.

Brown and Hazen had strong personal feelings about how the drug should be developed and used and to whom the profits should go. If they gave up the patent rights to their employer, they would have no say in the drug's development, marketing, and use. However, as individuals, they did not have the money to follow through on a patent application. To receive a patent for the drug, they would have to prove, through years of testing, that it was effective.

Fortunately, the two researchers were able to get help from the Research Corporation, which had been set up in 1912 to help the public benefit from scientific research. (You can read more about this corporation in Appendix 1.) The Research Corporation took care of the patent application for Hazen and Brown, using its resources to produce the drug in large quantities and in various forms and to conduct the necessary tests to prove that it worked. Brown and Hazen continued to have scientific input and control. The process of getting approval for nystatin took five years.

The patent was granted in Brown's and Hazen's names. However, they agreed to assign all their royalties (their share of the profits) to the Research Corporation. To get nystatin on the market, the Research Corporation licensed a drug manufacturing company, E.R. Squibb and Sons, to make and sell the drug for five years. As a licensee, Squibb returned a percentage of the profits to the Research Corporation.

Royalties received by the Research Corporation during the life of the patent came to more than thirteen million dollars. Half of the money went to support research in the physical sciences. The other half went to establish the Brown-Hazen Fund to support biomedical research. Squibb awarded Brown and Hazen its first five-thousand-dollar Squibb Award in Chemotherapy in 1955 in recognition of their discovery of the first broadly effective antifungal antibiotic safe for human use.

Nystatin also has proven useful in nonmedical ways. It destroys fungi that attack trees, such as Dutch elm disease. It keeps certain foods such as bananas and livestock feed from spoiling. And it has been used to restore valuable paintings damaged by mold.

Elizabeth Hazen died in 1975. Rachel Brown died five years later, in 1980.

*Nystatin was a major medical breakthrough because it kills the fungus without harming the essential bacteria in the body that control fungi. In other words, it does not have any bad side effects.*

◆ Research chemist Stephanie Kwolek holds laboratory equipment used in experiments for the DuPont Company. "Each day can be a new learning experience when you are doing research, and for me each day was just that," Kwolek says.

## IN HER WORDS . . .

Each of the women inventors interviewed for this section has received recognition for important work in her scientific field. These women tell us how their inventions came to be and how their curiosity about the world, their ambition, and circumstances led to achievement and personal fulfillment.

### *Stephanie Kwolek*

In a fairy tale, a miller's daughter is commanded by the king to spin straw into gold. A funny little man named Rumpelstiltskin comes to her aid. In the case of Stephanie Kwolek, a chemist for the DuPont Company, no odd little man showed up to help. But through persistence, she found a way to create an extremely lightweight fiber that feels like silk and looks like gold yet is stronger than steel.

DuPont calls the fiber Kevlar aramid. Its hundreds of uses include marine rope and oil-rig cable, canoe hulls and auto bodies, bullet-resistant vests, motorcycle helmets, automobile tires, boat sails, and spacecraft. Kwolek tells how she gradually fell in love with chemistry and about the discoveries that led to this new product.

"Not in a thousand years did I think I would be a chemist when I was a child," Kwolek says. "We lived near a wooded area in New Kensington, Pennsylvania. My father was a self-taught naturalist. I spent time in the woods with him identifying trees, bushes, and flowers. But I also liked designing and making clothes for dolls, including many paper dolls. I sewed on my mother's sewing machine beginning at the age of five. I made hundreds of dresses, coats, and whole outfits."

With the idea of someday becoming a medical doctor, she majored in chemistry at Carnegie-Mellon University, in Pittsburgh, Pennsylvania, with a minor in biology. Just after World War II, in 1946, she went to work for DuPont.

"For the first four years, my work was not very interesting. Then I went to a new laboratory in Wilmington, Delaware, where I began working with condensation polymers. The work was so interesting I gave up the idea of being a doctor."

Kwolek was working with certain **polymers** that are stiff and rodlike, with the hope of changing them into a form that could be spun into fibers. She experimented with various liquids to try to dissolve the polymers, but nothing seemed to work. Then she discovered that these polymers formed **liquid crystalline** solutions that were unlike any polymer solutions she had seen before.

**POLYMER**
A very large molecule. "Poly" means "many"; "polymer" means "many units of atoms." There are addition polymers and condensation polymers. An *addition polymer* is made by units of atoms sticking together to create the molecule. Nothing is eliminated. Synthetic rubber is an example of an addition polymer. A *condensation polymer* is formed by the elimination, or splitting out, of a small molecule, such as water. Thus, the polymer is reduced, or condensed, and we end up with a long chain of units bonded together. Nylon and Kevlar are condensation polymers.

**LIQUID CRYSTALLINE**
Crystals are structures and patterns in which atoms are connected. A pattern is repeated to build up a solid body, or crystal. For instance, a diamond is made up of crystals, each having the same structure and pattern, which is revealed in the shape of the diamond. A liquid crystal is crystal-like but fluid, so that it has properties of both a solid and a liquid.

*Kwolek found a way to create an extremely lightweight fiber that feels like silk and looks like gold yet is stronger than steel.*

**VISCOSITY**

The ease with which a fluid flows. Molasses, for instance, is sticky, or semifluid, and thus is highly viscous, or has a high viscosity. Water flows freely and so has a low viscosity.

**SPIN**

There are several ways to spin synthetic fibers. One way is to melt a polymer (see page 59) and force the liquid through tiny holes in a spinneret (a device used to spin fibers). The molten filaments are cooled and solidified as they travel to be collected on a bobbin. This is called *melt spinning*. Another way is to dissolve a polymer in a solvent and force the solution through the tiny holes in a spinneret and into a tube through which hot air circulates and carries off the solvent. The solidified filaments are wound on a bobbin. This is called *dry spinning*. There are other methods of spinning as well. The method used depends on the polymer with which the chemist is working.

"What I saw as unusual with the solution I created was its very low **viscosity.** Most polymer solutions are thick, more like syrup. This was more like water. The other unusual thing was that it was hazy — milky-looking. Most solutions are transparent. When I turned the beaker that contained the polymer solution, I noticed the solution became opalescent. When I looked at the polymer solution in a polarizing microscope, I saw areas of brilliant colors. With ordinary solutions, there is only darkness.

"Initially I had trouble convincing the technician in the semiworks area [a room with large equipment for larger-scale work] to **spin** the liquid crystalline polymer solutions because they were so unlike conventional polymer solutions. The milkiness and opalescence suggested the presence of solid particles in the solutions, and these particles had the potential to plug the tiny holes in the spinneret. To satisfy myself, I passed one of these solutions through a very fine filter. The filtrate, however, was still milky and opalescent. I now knew there were no solid particles. Although the liquid crystalline solutions were of very low viscosity, I was convinced that they were spinnable because of the presence of a certain cohesive quality.

"We dry-spun one of these polymer solutions with no difficulty, and the as-spun fibers were very strong and very stiff — in fact, considerably stiffer than glass fibers. I had these tensile property measurements repeated several times by the physical test laboratory before I passed this startling information to my colleagues.

"The research program was greatly expanded to include other related polymers and a number of other people. The work was kept very secret while patent applications were being written.

"In the development of a new product, no one person does everything. Kevlar is a very complex fiber, and many people participated in its development through further inventions, modifications, and the creation of new end-use applications.

"The downside of research is that one often faces frustrations. Sometimes the experiments don't work out. Many hours go into the final result of finding a polymer, dissolving, and spinning. You need the right combination of polymer-molecule weight, the right solvent, the right concentration of the polymer in the solvent, the right temperature. There are many variables to work out every step along the way. The most important factors in inventing are persistence and the ability to recognize something unusual."

Kwolek received a promotion and a bonus for her discovery. Her name is on the patent. She went on to become a research associate with DuPont and now serves as a consultant. She has been the author or coauthor of seventeen U.S. patents on polymers, polycondensation processes and liquid crystalline solutions, and fibers. In 1991, the Society for the

Advancement of Material and Process Engineering honored her with its George Lubin Memorial Award for meritorious achievement. The award was given in recognition of her achievements in working with chemical structures to create useful products.

Kwolek says that her main reward is the excitement of discovery. "Most chemists work all their lives and very hard, and never are able to participate in a discovery that has done so much good as Kevlar."

### Patsy O. Sherman

In 1952, Patsy O. Sherman was just out of college and on her first job as a chemist. She had been hired on a temporary basis by the 3M Company to help develop a kind of fuel hose that would not get mushy and break up when used with jet fuel. She and fellow researcher Samuel Smith were making rubber in latex form with a new synthetic material, a fluorochemical, hoping that it would be the answer.

"We were not successful," Sherman says. "The material tended to get stiff and brittle in cold temperatures. But while we were experimenting, someone in the lab spilled a sample of this new compound on her tennis shoes. It's a milk-like substance, like the sap that comes from the rubber tree. It could not be removed. Soap wouldn't wet it. Solvent wouldn't wet it. We thought, 'Wouldn't it make a wonderful treatment for fabrics!'

"As a result, my job was no longer temporary. I began working with fluorochemicals to treat fabrics. It took seven years before we had a commercial success. We made many other discoveries along the way."

It was worth the wait. The 3M Company earned millions of dollars on the product, which has the trademark Scotchgard, and on other products that followed from the research. Scotchgard has been called a textile miracle of the modern world. The compound is used worldwide to repel soil from sofas, chairs, tablecloths, clothing, and other objects that we use every

◆ Chemist Patsy Sherman believes that women are naturally creative. Her name appears on sixteen patents awarded to the 3M Company, including one for Scotchgard.

day. Sometimes it is put on fabric in the factory, or you can buy a can and spray it on yourself. The protective coating means that people have to do much less washing and cleaning and that fabrics wear and look nice much longer.

Sherman grew up in Minnesota at a time when women were usually discouraged from going into professions other than teaching or nursing. "In high school in 1947, the counselor asked what we wanted to be after graduation," she says. "I said, 'A nuclear physicist.' He picked me as the most confused of all the people in the class.

"When World War II ended, there was a test given to returning servicemen and later adapted for high school students to find out what strong interests we had. One version was for males, one for females. I took the female version, and it showed that the only thing I was fit for was to be a housewife. I said, 'I am not going to college to become a housewife! Besides, what if nobody wants to marry me?' So they gave me the male version. This showed that I should be a chemist.

"I studied no chemistry in high school, but I majored in chemistry and math in college. There were only one or two other women in these courses. That suited me fine. I liked boys just as much as I liked molecules." Sherman graduated from Gustavus Adolphus College, in St. Peter, Minnesota, in 1952 with a bachelor of arts degree.

"My father was influential in my career. He never graduated from high school but was self-taught. He had an inquisitive nature. He would bring home puzzles for me to work out. Once he brought a little glass bird. It would lean over and put its beak in water, then come back up. We couldn't see what made it move. 'How does it work?' he asked me.

"The head is slightly heavier than the tail, which makes it tip over. The tail contains a wick, which draws water. When the bird leans forward and dips its beak in water, the water is wicked to the tail, and this makes the tail heavier and the bird stand erect. After a time, the water evaporates, so that the head is heavier again and falls back into the water.

"My father talked a chemist into giving him basic lab equipment to experiment with. We distilled water on the kitchen stove. But we built a closed system. No air could get in, and when it was heated, it blew up. Water and glass were all over our ceiling and the rest of the kitchen."

Sherman's and Samuel Smith's names are on sixteen patents awarded to 3M for their work. Both have received many honors and awards for their

*"A lot of new discoveries are accidental," Patsy Sherman says. In her case, a ruined tennis shoe meant a big breakthrough in fabric protection.*

creative efforts in the field of chemistry. Sherman was inducted into the Minnesota Inventors Hall of Fame in 1989. She retired from 3M in 1992.

"Women are naturally inventive," she says. "A woman will nearly always change a recipe rather than use it just the way it is written. And women can always find a dozen other uses for products besides what they were originally intended for."

### Gertrude Elion

Some of the most impressive work done by women in chemistry has been in the field of medicine. Gertrude Elion was a major contributor in the development of "wonder drugs" that have saved thousands of lives. She, along with George Hitchings, received the **Nobel Prize** for medicine in 1988. With her name on forty-five medical patents, she became the first woman inducted into the National Inventors Hall of Fame in 1991.

"'What am I going to do? What shall I be?' These are the questions I asked myself when I was growing up in the Bronx area of New York City," Elion says. "From the time I was small, I knew that I wanted to be self-reliant and not depend on anyone. My brother and I were given to understand that we ought to go into some profession.

"My father was a dentist. His office was part of our family's apartment in the Bronx. For a time, our living room and his waiting room were one and the same. We didn't have a lot of privacy. There weren't many times we could all sit down and eat together. Our family life was mixed with the dental practice. I knew all of the patients, and they knew me. Some brought me candy.

"The joke about me was 'Gertrude is always worried about the future.' Whenever anyone gave me anything, I always kept some of it back 'for tomorrow.'

"My mother came to the United States from Russia when she was fourteen and married at nineteen. She was particularly anxious for me to have a career. She was ahead of her time concerning ideas about what women should do. When she was young, it was not considered proper for a woman to want to do what was thought to be men's work.

"When I was sixteen, my grandfather died of stomach cancer. It was a long, painful illness. After watching him die, I knew what I had to do. It had to be something to do with cancer."

Elion's good grades got her into Hunter College, in New York City. "It was free, a fortunate thing, because this was during the 1930s, when the great economic depression was causing hardship for most people. My father was barely making a living in his dental practice because his

**NOBEL PRIZE**
Each year, Nobel Prizes are awarded to individuals for outstanding work for the benefit of humanity. They are given in several areas of science, economics, literature, and world peace. A famous Swedish chemist, Alfred Bernhard Nobel, who died in 1896, established the awards in his will.

patients had no money to pay him."

Elion graduated from Hunter with high honors. Even so, it was years before she was able to work on cancer. Jobs were scarce. When she applied to research laboratories, she was told, "'We never had a woman before. It might be distracting to the men.' Or 'If we hire you, you'll get married soon and leave.' I was stubborn. I refused to be told I couldn't do it."

While going to graduate school at night, Elion taught school and later worked for a food-processing plant analyzing foods. "'This is not what I want to do,' I told myself. So I quit my job and found something else."

The chance for women to get better jobs came with World War II. Elion found a position as research assistant to George Hitchings at Burroughs

◆ Nobel Prize–winner Gertrude Elion's name is on forty-five medical patents. One of the drugs she helped develop has saved the lives of many children with leukemia, a cancer of the blood. Here she is shown on vacation with a grandniece and three grandnephews.

Wellcome Research Laboratories, a company that makes and sells drugs. He was studying the nature of cancer cells and how they differ from normal cells. "I was fascinated. There was no question that this would be my lifework." The two have worked as a team for thirty years.

Cells are the basic units that make up the human body. Cancer cells are "outlaw" cells that grow and destroy healthy cells. The problem with many drugs that kill cancer cells is that they also harm healthy cells. Hitchings and Elion wanted to create a chemical compound that would kill cancer cells without damaging normal cells.

*"My advice to young people is don't be afraid to ask how things work. If we don't have curiosity, we don't have science. Also, if you are not satisfied with one job, be brave enough to look for a different one."*

"We tested a whole series of compounds. It is not often known ahead of time which disease a new drug will affect. Some may work on viruses; some may work on malaria. You need to have a hunch. What do normal cells contain? What if we replace the oxygen on one of the cell's building blocks with a sulfur? How will that change the reactions in the cell?" After years of research, Hitchings and Elion made Purinethol and Thioquinne, two important drugs for treating acute leukemia (cancer of the blood).

The researchers also created Imuram, a drug that helps prevent the body's rejection of a transplanted kidney. "When you meet someone who has lived for twenty-five years with a kidney graft, there's your reward," says Elion, who also has helped find treatments for gout, rheumatoid arthritis, and herpes virus infections.

For sixteen years before her retirement in 1983, Elion headed the Department of Experimental Therapy at Burroughs Wellcome in Research Triangle Park, North Carolina. She remains active in research and in many professional organizations.

What is the difference between discovery and invention in medicine? "I consider science a process of discovery. Inventing is part of discovery," Elion says. "We are inventing if we create a new compound, something that never existed before. Discovery is finding a use for it.

"We need to nurture curiosity in our schools. When we do experiments, we should say, 'What do you think will happen?' rather than telling them what the outcome will be. Students should be doing experiments to find out something, not to prove something.

"My advice to young people is don't be afraid to ask how things work. If we don't have curiosity, we don't have science. Also, if you are not satisfied with one job, be brave enough to look for a different one."

### Yuri Yamamoto

In 1991, the B. F. Goodrich Company and the National Invention Center started the first national competition to encourage and recognize creative and inventive problem solving by college students. The winner of the first award in the plant category was Yuri Yamamoto, then a student at North Carolina State University. She received five thousand dollars and national recognition of her work.

Bugs, salt, metals, and other things in soil can harm plants. Every year, farmers lose millions of dollars because of diseases and insects that attack the roots of their crops. Plant biologists have been experimenting with genes to make plants stronger. Some plants have great genetic resistance to diseases and pests. Scientists know how to fuse genes from one plant to another, but adding genes to a food plant to make it resistant to diseases or bugs also might make the plant harmful to people who use it.

Yamamoto's invention, developed with her university advisor, Mark Conkling, is called the Root Specific Gene Promoter. Yamamoto and Conkling learned how to add a gene in such a way that it is active only in

♦ Yuri Yamamoto examines cell material grown in her laboratory at North Carolina State University, where she is a research associate. Her prize-winning work with the tobacco plant could have far-reaching effects for human welfare.

*"Children often think scientists are people who*
*do weird experiments that are not practical. They only*
*understand the importance if they can see the results right away.*
*But what is learned from the experiments may be useful in the future.*
*It could be one hundred or two hundred years later.*
*That is the importance of doing basic research."*

the roots of a plant and thus not harmful to people who use other parts of the plant.

"I really like to play with plants," Yamamoto says. "They have very interesting features. If you cut down even a large part of a plant, the plant will often grow back. In some cases, you can reduce a plant to a single cell, and the plant will grow out of this single cell. We people have trouble healing even a little cut!

"I said I wanted to study agriculture in college. My family was not so sure about this. My mother said, 'If you want to study agriculture, marry a farmer.' I didn't know what the study of agriculture was about, and neither did she. But I was very interested in agriculture because it produces food, which is the most important thing for people."

Yamamoto, who was born and raised in Japan, worked on a dairy farm when she was in high school. "We had to get up early and milk the cows. I remember doing it when there was still snow on the ground. I enjoyed the work so much that I often went to farms to help — or bother! — farmers when I was an undergraduate student. I still hope that I can live on a farm someday."

Yamamoto studied animal science at Kyoto University before coming to the United States in 1984. "I married and came to be with my husband, who was in North Carolina, and to go to graduate school. I was interested in animal development, so I started in a graduate program in the School of Veterinary Medicine at North Carolina State University.

"I had long been interested in reproduction. I started working with some hormones in chickens. Then I studied molecular biology in a laboratory course. The instructor was a young assistant professor who was beginning plant molecular biology research. Talking to him, I became very interested in plants.

"The plant that I started studying in the laboratory was tobacco. It was one of the best tools for studying molecular biology at that time because it was one of the few species that we could genetically engineer. We thought it would be interesting to work with the root part of the plant because the root of a plant is the site of many interactions with the soil and soil-borne organisms. We were not trying to prevent anything. Later we saw ways that a 'promoter' could be used.

"As I have said, every single cell has two complete sets of genes to make an organism. These genes are tightly regulated so that only a subset of genes are active in a particular cell type at a particular time of development. For example, the red or white color gene of a flower is active only in flower petals but not in other parts of the plant. The gene promoter plays an important role in this type of regulation. It is a specific area of a gene that regulates the correct expression pattern [when to be active and when to be silent]. Now we know that if we take this promoter region away from other parts of the gene and fuse it to another gene, the new gene will be under the control of the fused promoter.

"Roots are affected by bacteria in the dirt and by some insects. For example, one parasite that can harm a plant through its roots is the nematode. In the future, someone may be able to find a gene that makes a plant resistant to the nematode. For instance, the gene may produce a substance that kills the parasite. This new gene could be fused to the root-specific promoter and the whole thing put back into the plant. Then we could grow the plant, and its roots would be resistant to the parasite. The other parts of the plant would be pretty much normal. Every cell of the engineered plant would contain the new structure, but the fused genes would be active only in the roots. It would be silent in other parts of the plant."

Yamamoto received a Ph.D. in **genetics** from North Carolina State University and has done research in plant molecular biology at Yale University. To what does she attribute her motivation to excel?

"I grew up without television, and I believe that has a lot to do with my going into science. I never had a moment to be bored. I was very busy. I loved to read, play musical instruments, and play outside. Children have a very good imagination — they are the best inventors. Why do so many lose it? They are given so many things that they don't have to invent anything.

"Children often think scientists are people who do weird experiments that are not practical. They only understand the importance if they can see the results right away. But what is learned from the experiments may be useful in the future. It could be one hundred or two hundred years later. That is the importance of doing **basic research.**"

**GENETICS**
The study of genes (see page 48).

**BASIC RESEARCH**
Sometimes called "pure research." Scientific investigation out of a desire for general knowledge, as opposed to working toward a specific goal or purpose.

# ACTIVITIES

## Project 1

## SAVE THE WORLD

**Objective**
Students use problem-solving skills such as inferring, predicting, and analyzing. Students learn to see a problem from many viewpoints.

People say, "We can't solve the problems of the world." Why not? This exercise lets you work on a major world problem.

**1.** Brainstorm a list of problems facing humankind. Choose one and put it in the center of a wheel, as shown in the example. You will need more than one sheet of paper, but start with just one.

**2.** Brainstorm a list of solutions that would involve some area of technology. Don't worry if your solutions are "impossible." Put the solutions on the wheel in one of the circles.

**3.** Choose one of the solutions and brainstorm again to find problems with this solution. Put the problems in appropriately placed circles, as shown in the example.

**4.** Pick one of the problems with this solution. Brainstorm ways to overcome this problem. Add these to the wheel. Don't hesitate to use other "impossible" solutions.

Your wheel will probably become lopsided. Why? Because you have not had time to fill in all the possibilities. But given time and patience and with enough people thinking, there actually might be a workable solution to the problem.

☞ Example
1. Problem: Millions of people get sick or die from contaminated water.

2. Brainstorm solutions.

☞ Install a built-in filter or purification system in a person's body at birth.
☞ Purify the water people drink.
☞ Use another drink besides water.
☞ Make the human body so that it doesn't need water.
☞ Make a cup that kills germs.
☞ Make people boil their water.

☞ Find the source of contamination and stop it.

3. Choose one solution and brainstorm the problems with it or the questions it raises. Solution: Make a cup that kills germs.

☞ What germ killers could you use?
☞ How would you get the germ killers in the cup?
☞ How would you distribute the cups to everyone?

4. Choose one problem in number 3 and brainstorm solutions to it. Problem: How would you distribute the cups to everyone?

When you run out of space, take one of your solutions in number 2, such as "Make a cup that kills germs," and put it in the center of another blank sheet of paper. Start a new wheel.

The examples given are purposely far-out. The idea is to show that creative thinkers cannot censor the mind or ignore any avenue of thought. Disease caused by contaminated water is a complex issue for which technology can be only one part of the solution. To consider this question in a serious way, you could research which areas of technology — chemistry, engineering, and so on — offer hope.

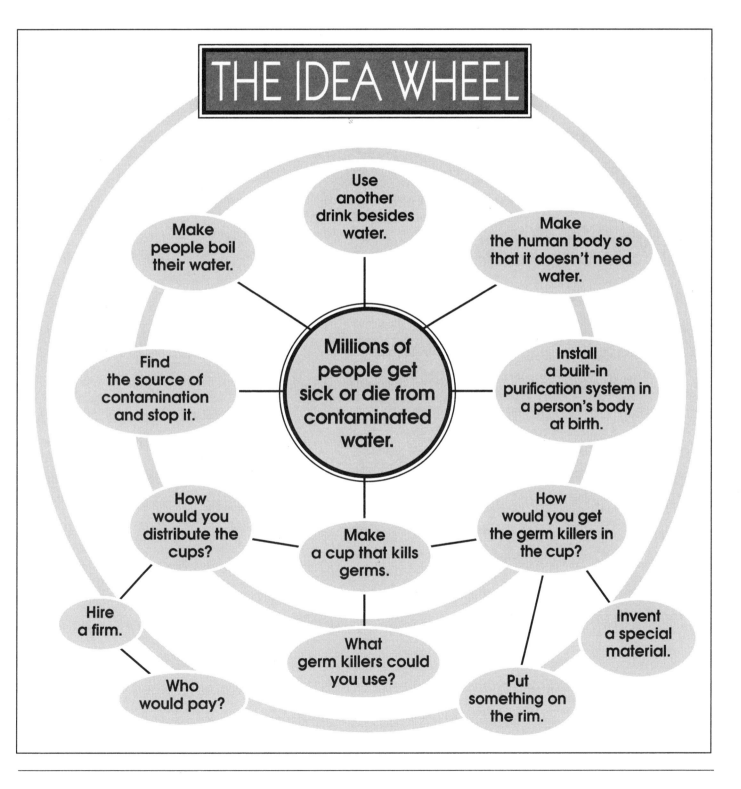

# THE IDEA WHEEL

Millions of people get sick or die from contaminated water.

Use another drink besides water.

Make people boil their water.

Make the human body so that it doesn't need water.

Find the source of contamination and stop it.

Install a built-in purification system in a person's body at birth.

How would you distribute the cups?

Make a cup that kills germs.

How would you get the germ killers in the cup?

Hire a firm.

Who would pay?

What germ killers could you use?

Put something on the rim.

Invent a special material.

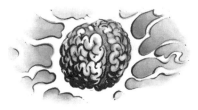

## *Project 2*

## TRICKS OF MEMORY

**Objective**
To use the pleasures of sound and rhythm in the tasks of learning and remembering.

Dance, drama, and poetry are entertaining, but they are also ways we preserve the memory of important people and events in history or myth. Suppose you are afraid that the names of women inventors will be forgotten in the future. How could you plant their names in the minds of children?

☞ Join with a partner to make up a simple rhyme, or jingle, that young children could sing, using the name of an inventor mentioned in this chapter. Then share your jingles as a class. Notice how the rhymes differ!

☞ Alternatively, if you enjoy playing with words, compose rhymes for several inventors and share them with the class.

## *Puzzle 1*

## WHO **WAS** THAT WOMAN?

**Across**

**2.** According to Elion, scientific investigators sometimes follow a _____ if they are not sure what disease a drug might affect.

**5.** Sherman's invention is used to treat fabrics so that they

_____ _____.

**7.** _____ Sherman discovered a fabric treatment after some of the substances she was working with accidentally spilled.

**10.** Yamamoto added a _____ to enable a plant's roots to resist pests and diseases.

**12.** Today most inventing is done by _____ _____, not by individuals working alone.

**15.** Benerito's invention made the _____ nearly obsolete.

**17.** Stephanie _____ helped develop a fiber that looks like gold and feels like silk.

**18.** Yuri _____ worked on a dairy farm as a teenager.

**Down**

**1.** When Sherman took the male version of an aptitude test in high school, it indicated that she should become a _____.

**3.** An important quality for an inventor to have is _____.

**4.** Gertrude _____ developed many medicines.

**6.** Benerito developed an intravenous _____ _____ to feed people who cannot eat.

**7.** Kwolek worked with large molecules called _____ to develop a substance that could be spun into fibers.

**8.** Ruth _____ is the author or coauthor of more than fifty patents, many of which deal with fabrics.

**9.** _____ was the codesigner of the country's first electronic telephone switching system.

**11.** Hopper invented the first widely used computer _____ to enable people to instruct computers to do useful tasks.

**13.** One reason Hopper's inventions were not patented is because computer _____ had not yet come under patent protection.

**14.** The nickname of the "mother" of the U.S. Navy's computerized data system was _____ Grace.

**16.** The name of the computer language invented by Hopper is _____.

# WHO *WAS* THAT WOMAN?

**Answers on page 159.**

*Puzzle 2*

## RELATING THE GENERAL TO THE SPECIFIC

Review the stories about Grace Hopper, Elizabeth Hazen and Rachel Brown, Patsy Sherman, and Stephanie Kwolek. Then match the general statements in the left-hand column with the specific statements in the right-hand column.

_____ **1.** Sometimes when researchers are looking for an answer to one problem, they accidentally find an answer to another problem they weren't even thinking about at the time. They must use their imagination.

_____ **2.** When some people hear the words "You can't do that because it has never been done," they don't even try to solve a problem in a new way. But an inventive person will say, "That's no reason!" She or he will go right ahead and do the "impossible."

_____ **3.** A researcher is considered an inventor if she or he solves a problem that leads to the development of a new product. Other members of a research team might solve additional problems before the new product can be made. Therefore, several people often share the credit for most modern scientific inventions.

_____ **4.** In medicine, a major problem is developing drugs that can treat one part of the body without having side effects on another part of the body.

**Answers on page 159.**

**a.** Researchers Rachel Brown and Elizabeth Hazen created a drug called nystatin. It was a major medical breakthrough because it kills fungal infections without harming the essential bacteria in the body that control fungi.

**b.** Patsy Sherman was trying to develop a material for making fuel hoses when a chemical solution spilled on a shoe. When the stuff wouldn't come off, Sherman had an idea for how to use the solution in a practical way. The result was Scotchgard, a fabric protector manufactured by the 3M Company.

**c.** When Grace Hopper began working with the Navy's computers, she was told that it was impossible for a computer to operate with instructions given in ordinary words such as "stop" and "execute." Yet she was successful in developing COBOL, the most widely used computer business language in the world.

**d.** Stephanie Kwolek was a research scientist for DuPont when she created a chemical solution that could be spun into strong, lightweight fibers. Other inventions and modifications by other DuPont researchers resulted in the development of a new "miracle fiber," which the company called Kevlar.

## *Think About It*

**Objective**
Students use different kinds of thinking skills, especially comparing, analyzing, and predicting.

**1.** The U.S. Navy built the first large digital computer, Mark I, in the early 1940s. How are modern computers different from it? How do they differ in size? In capabilities? How can it be that as computers become more powerful, they also become smaller?

**2.** Computers can be programmed to create a situation on the computer screen that is similar to a real-life situation. Sometimes this is called virtual reality. We know that airplane pilots first learn to control a plane by going into a simulated cockpit and being put in simulated flight situations. How could this type of computer program help inventors?

**3.** Kevlar is very strong but also lightweight. Researchers have found hundreds of uses for it. What new uses can you think of for this product?

**4.** Many inventions make a significant difference in people's lives. How did Gertrude Elion make a difference? Patsy Sherman? Ruth Benerito?

**5.** Look around you. What inventions do you see? How would your world be different had one of these inventions not been made?

☞ Examples: rubber, hinges, the ability to shape metal, paper, radio, cotton wash-and-wear clothing

**6.** Watch an episode of *Star Trek*. What "inventions" used on the *Enterprise* have not yet been invented in real life? How would you develop the fictional technologies shown?

**7.** Imagine the year 2094. What inventions might make schools, hospitals, and homes different from the way they are today?

## *The Way You See It*

**Objective**
Suggestions for writing assignments. Exercises in comparing and analyzing and in using research facilities.

**1.** Chemists use knowledge of natural products to create products that have similar qualities. What makes wool warmer than cotton? Think of ways this knowledge can be used to create a warm material using no wool.

**2.** Yuri Yamamoto is a scientist interested in agriculture. She received a Ph.D. in genetics. What does this knowledge have to do with farming? In what other professions or lines of work might knowledge about genes and the ability to change them be helpful?

**3.** Amelia Bloomer is another designer who has a special place in history. Find some books or articles about her and explain how she contributed to women's freedom. (One source is the October 1985 issue of *COBBLESTONE* magazine on clothing.)

**4.** Research the history of the Equal Rights Amendment. Give arguments for and against the amendment. What side are you on?

**5.** What do the women you read about in this chapter have in common? List at least three things.

**6.** This book begins with a short story about a girl who can spin glass. Does it remind you of the work of Katharine Blodgett and Stephanie Kwolek? They, too, performed magic by achieving what others could not imagine. Write a fictional story that focuses on the invention of someone you read about in this chapter. Make sure your story shows how creativity is a kind of "magic."

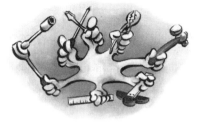

*Imagine That!*

**Objective**
To learn by doing, with cross-curriculum application.

**1. Doing basic research.** As a class, investigate an object without any idea of trying to use the information for a specific use. You might investigate all the properties of a rubber band, for instance. Ask these questions: How far will it stretch without breaking? How does it change if heated to a certain temperature? If cooled to a certain temperature? If wet? If greasy? The idea is not to figure out ways to use the object but to know as much about it as possible.

**2. Applying the knowledge.** Take all the information found in the previous exercise. How could you apply some of this knowledge in a practical way? In new ways? Give several examples.

**3. What is the question?** Where invention and problem solving are concerned, asking the right question can be as important as having the right answer. For this exercise, brainstorm to choose a problem that most students have in common. Then brainstorm questions surrounding this problem. Allow no possible solutions, only questions.

For example, propose this problem: We are overloaded with information. Then ask these questions: Why? Who says we have to know everything? Is there such a thing as information overload? Is there a way to focus on one problem? Is there a way to use information without being overwhelmed?

**4. Testing!** Kevlar is a human-made fiber that is lightweight but has a tensile strength greater than steel. (The tensile strength of a fiber refers to how much energy it would take to pull it apart.) Gather several different fibers such as cotton, polyester, nylon, silk, and hemp. Let two individuals try to pull each fiber apart. List the fibers in order of their tensile strengths, starting with the strongest.

**5. Pass it on.** In the process of invention, one person's idea often inspires another person to invent something that is related. Play the "Pass It On" game as part of an inventing exercise.

☞ Divide up into a few groups. Each group will design a contraption using a certain number of items that can be found around the home or classroom — for example, wheels, rubber bands, mousetraps, paper clips, bottles, and springs. All the groups should have the same items. The contraption should perform some action — for example, a marble chute might take the marbles along various paths, separate them, drop them, and so on.

☞ Then pass it on! The groups exchange contraptions, and each group is given a certain amount of time to add to the original invention and improve on it. Students may use whatever tools, items, or

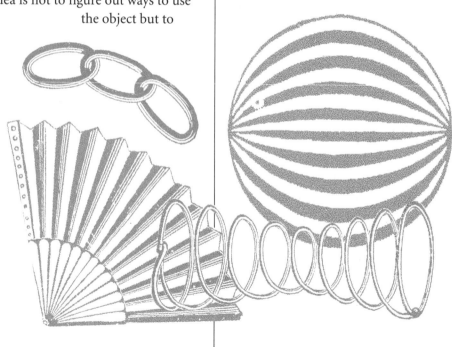

devices they find in the classroom.

**6. Make yogurt.** Sometimes we forget how much chemistry is part of our everyday lives. But as soon as we eat and digest our food, we become living chemistry experiments. When we cook, we're doing chemistry. Making yogurt not only lets us watch chemistry in progress but also gives us something to eat and shows us how bacteria can work for our benefit.

**Note:** Usually you are told exactly what equipment you need for an experiment. This time, part of the challenge is for you to come up with your own list of equipment. In some cases, you might have to improvise, or even invent something that you need to carry out the tasks. If you want to double-check your equipment before you start, a list of recommended equipment is included in the "Answers" section on page 159.

The bacteria species in yogurt are *Streptococcus thermophilus* and *Lactobacillus bulgaricus.* Enzymes produced by these bacteria interact with the sugar naturally present in milk, causing lactic acid fermentation. That is, the enzymes cause the milk to curdle, a process of breaking down compounds in the milk. The result (if all goes well) will be yogurt.

☞ Divide up into small groups, each of which will make a batch of yogurt. When you are finished, compare the groups' results. If any batches look or smell odd or don't

get firm, toss them out and share the ones that look and taste okay.

☞ Follow these steps for each batch:

**a.** Empty half a pint of milk into a pot and add 1/2 cup of dried milk.

**b.** Heat the mixture to 199°F to 205°F — just below boiling. Stir to keep from burning. Watch the temperature carefully. When the mixture reaches the correct temperature, remove it from the heat and let cool to 99°F to 104°F.

**c.** Pour the mixture back into the milk carton or into a sterile jar. Add 1 to 2 teaspoons of good-quality, fresh, unflavored yogurt.

**d.** Label and cover the container. Place it and the other groups' containers in another container that is large enough to hold them all. This container must be heated or insulated in some way to keep the temperature inside at 99°F to 104°F. *This is crucial!* The mixtures cannot cool down or heat up too much.

**e.** After 6 to 8 hours, remove the containers and put them in a refrigerator or an ice chest. Chill for several hours or overnight.

**f.** If you wish, add fruit or nuts to the firm yogurt and eat.

**7. Research activity.** After graduating from high school, Nobel Prize–winner Gertrude Elion attended Hunter College in New York City. She was able to attend this college because it was free. Do

any institutions today provide a free college education? What kinds of scholarships are available for students who cannot afford to pay? Research these questions using your school library and guidance office.

*You Say Yes;
I Say No*

**Objective**
Topics for debate.

**1.** The United States should not use taxpayers' money to support scientific research unless it is directed toward solving a specific problem. Do you agree or disagree?

**2.** If you want to keep your grades high and you think you are not good in math, you should avoid math classes. Do you agree or disagree?

# 4 THE SKY IS NOT

◆ Barbara Askins's award-winning photographic development process brought out detail in pictures taken from above the earth that otherwise would have been useless.

THE NATIONAL AERONAUTICS AND SPACE ADMINISTRATION (NASA) works to expand human knowledge of the earth and its environment, the solar system, and the universe. Its explorers are not just astronauts who go out into space but men and women who probe the unknown with the latest technical instruments and who invent new instruments to make gathering more information possible.

Some of the women who work from field centers here on earth have wanted to be astronauts since childhood and hope to be chosen for flights. In this chapter, seven women inventors in the space program talk about their ideas, how they became part of NASA, and how they feel about their work.

## BARBARA ASKINS:
## MAKING THE INVISIBLE VISIBLE

In 1975, some astronomical and earth observation photographs taken by NASA researchers did not have enough detail to tell researchers very much. Some of them contained important astronomical information and general information about our planet. NASA scientists knew that the images were on the film — if only they could find some way to make them visible!

This was the first assignment given to Barbara Askins, a research chemist hired by the Marshall Space Flight Center in Huntsville, Alabama, in 1975. After two years of studying film chemistry and conducting laboratory research, Askins discovered a new method of developing film using radioactive materials. Her invention is called the autoradiograph. She was

# THE LIMIT

National Inventor of the Year in 1978 and NASA Inventor of the Year.

"'What is it?' I remember asking when I was in the seventh grade in the little town of Petersburg, Tennessee," Askins says. "Other children were saying, 'Oh, my gosh, this year we have to study science! It's so hard!'

"Much to my surprise, when I started studying, I found out I liked science. My teacher, Mr. Thurman Cobb, helped us relate science to the ordinary world by talking about things such as atmospheric pressure and what it has to do with the weight of air. We also studied chicken embryos and how they developed.

"In high school, I enjoyed chemistry classes but thought I should be an English major. I expected to be a teacher. It seemed more like what girls should do. I didn't know anyone who was a scientist."

Later, at Middle Tennessee State College, Askins enrolled in a chemistry course "just for fun." After the first semester, she changed her major from English to chemistry. She fell in love with her chemistry lab instructor, quit school, and married him. When their two children started school, she enrolled at the University of Alabama in Huntsville, earned a B.S. in chemistry, and began teaching high school physics.

"My first contact with NASA was when I took students on field trips to the Marshall Space Flight Center in Huntsville. I wanted to inspire the students, but I inspired myself. I became dissatisfied with reading and talking about science. I wanted to do it." She went back to the University of Alabama to get a master's degree and applied for a job in the space program.

"To my amazement, NASA hired me! My first assignment, under the supervision of Dr. C.R. O'Dell, was to try to find a way to enhance, or make clearer, astronomical photographs. These photographs are often underexposed. I was given underexposed earth resource images as test images and worked with old photographs from a museum in Birmingham. Two years later, I got successful results.

"I worked hard on that first assignment, putting in many hours. I would go to the lab, put on something to process, and get books that I thought might help me. If my work depended on the delivery of new equipment, instead of waiting for it to come, I would borrow or scrounge what I needed.

"I read a lot of chemistry and theory to see what approaches might be eliminated. To enhance the photographic image, I had to find a chemical that would combine with silver but not with the emulsion. I studied film chemistry.

*" 'What is it?' I remember asking when I was in the seventh grade in the little town of Petersburg, Tennessee,"* Askins says. *"Other children were saying, 'Oh, my gosh, this year we have to study science! It's so hard!' "*

"I was working on my own in the lab and had to do everything. Since I was using radioactive materials, I had to be extremely careful. I spent a lot of time thoroughly washing beakers, flasks, and other lab equipment. I was on my feet constantly. It was hard work, but it didn't seem like it then.

"I had some real failures, too. Once I left a solution in the laboratory, where it got too hot. It ruined one-of-a-kind emulsions. I will never forget climbing up the steps to my boss's office to report what had happened."

But success came with persistence. "I still remember that day in 1976. I took the film I was going to enhance, treated it to make it radioactive, and put it in a cassette in contact with a new piece of film. I let the new film be exposed by the radioactivity from the original film and waited several hours. I got the new film, took it out in the dark, and put it in the developer and fixative, like an ordinary photograph.

"It was a Friday afternoon. I was working in a small, special lab I had borrowed. I put this new film in the developer, in the stop, in the fixative. I looked at it. There it was! I had a good clear version of the test image, without significant background fog."

For her work, Askins received an award that earned her four thousand dollars, a promotion, and respect. She moved from research to project management and took part in the early planning for a space station. A very important use of her initial research today is for biological research. Scientists use autoradiographs to look at cells.

Since 1987, Askins has worked in the Office of Space Flight's Advanced Program Development Division. She manages a project called The Assured Crew Return Vehicle — a future program dedicated to the space station. The vehicle will be based at the space station to return ill or injured astronauts or to return astronauts in case of major problems with the space station or the shuttle.

"I would say to young people, don't make up your mind too early. You need good skills in math and English to succeed in almost any field. For me, math was not easy but was doable. I worked at it and was good enough. English may be more important than math because no matter how good you are in math, you have to be able to communicate. But in science, you need math in order to have something to communicate.

"Don't foreclose any option. Be anything, do anything you want to. Try everything — not just chemistry, but art, history, geography. Do your best. Delve into the subject. Do reading on the side. Find out what it's all about.

"Of course, somewhere along the way, you have to specialize and really go full blast in one area of concentration. But even then, don't underestimate the value of knowledge in seemingly unrelated fields. Don't ever pass up an opportunity to learn anything, anywhere!"

## JANE MALIN: PREPARING FOR THE UNEXPECTED

"There is a novel situation on every space flight," says research psychologist and engineer Jane

*Over the years, Jane Malin has been responsible for many NASA projects involving computer systems and human problem solving and decision-making.*

Malin of the Lyndon B. Johnson Space Center in Houston, Texas. "Something goes wrong, and nothing in the manual tells you what to do."

For example, on one space flight, astronauts were preparing the robot arm to open a damaged sun shield on a satellite. An alarm sounded. Warning lights came on. The astronauts traced the problem to a loss of electrical power in the robot's "elbow" joint. Ground controllers advised them to use the mechanical brake rather than the electronic control of the arm. Without electronic control, the arm could not push very hard on the sun shield. The astronauts tried to push the shield with the weak arm, but the shield would not move.

The ground controllers could see on a monitor that the joints of the arm were lined up in such a way that the elbow would not wobble as the astronauts pushed. They decided to use the electronic control in spite of the loss of power in the joint. As a result, the arm was able to push harder, and they were able to open the sun shield.

This situation turned out all right because the ground controllers could see what needed to be done. But what if they did not have enough information in a more complex case? To guarantee sophisticated analysis support in future situations, Malin and her colleagues developed the Discrete Event Simulation Tool for Analysis of Qualitative Models of Continuous Processing Systems, which NASA patented in 1990. Design engineers and ground controllers can use this software to design spacecraft and instruments and to solve unexpected problems during missions.

"The ground controllers in the case of the robot arm had to puzzle out new procedures, on the spot, and still get the job done," Malin says. "Now, when the ground controllers operating the shuttle need to figure out something gone wrong, they can turn to the analysis tool and see if their 'work around' will actually work, instead of having to do it all in their heads.

"In space flight, there may be no time for second tries. A delicate instrument might be lost or broken unless the problem is solved quickly. To help in unexpected situations, the way computers operate should correspond to the way humans operate, so the ground controllers can readily change codes or easily understand results.

"The invention also will be helpful to design engineers in the early stages. Non–computer scientists can alter and use the software. If they find out something new, they can put it in the software model. They won't have to go to a software group and get it six months later. Knowledge gained in design and testing can be made available to the ground controllers and the astronauts."

Malin was born in Tulsa, Oklahoma, in 1945. She grew up in Oklahoma and Ohio. "It took me a long time to find out what I was meant to do," she says. "I came from a family who knew nothing about engineering. I was trained in a liberal arts college and took no engineering courses. Computers were just appearing on college campuses when I was in school. At the University of Michigan, I hooked up with a graduate advisor who was strong in artificial intelligence. It seemed to me, at that time, that artificial intelligence had more to say about how people solve problems than did psychology."

Malin received a Ph.D. in experimental psychology from the University of Michigan in 1973, specializing in human cognition, or thinking patterns. She investigated how humans solve problems and helped develop computer programs using that knowledge. After graduating, she taught at the University of Houston, in Texas.

"I was an oddball. I got in trouble because of my interest in designing, which is not what I was supposed to be doing. But I realized I liked design — inventing and understanding requirements for systems. Ten years later, as I worked at NASA developing intelligent systems, I came to realize that I was best suited to be an engineer."

Malin started out working for NASA as a statistician, then became more involved in computer technology. Over the years, she has been responsible for many NASA projects involving computer systems and human problem solving and decision-making. She is a leader in the advanced group for research and development in the Intelligence Systems Branch of the Automation and Robotics Division, Engineering Directorate, at the Johnson Space Center.

Malin and her husband, a biological psychologist, have one daughter, who was born in 1986. They deliberately put off having a child until Malin had established her position at NASA.

"My daughter wishes I would stay home more with her, but she also takes pride in what I do. Does she want to follow in my footsteps? Well, right now, she wants to be a veterinarian because she loves animals. But she likes computer learning software.

"I have the problem of most working mothers — finding enough time, trying to be a supermom. I had the fear that once I had a child, my rate of productivity at work might go down. But this has not happened. I enjoy having a child, and I continue to expand and grow in my job."

*"In space flight, there may be no time for second tries. A delicate instrument might be lost or broken unless the problem is solved quickly. To help in unexpected situations, the way computers operate should correspond to the way humans operate, so the ground controllers can readily change codes or easily understand results."*

◆ Jeanne Crews is shown here with her Hypervelocity Impact Shield.

## JEANNE CREWS: A GUARD AGAINST SPACE POLLUTION

Junk traveling at tremendous speeds through space is a real problem. It is research engineer Jeanne Crews's job to make sure this junk does not hurt a spacecraft. Junk, or debris, comes from meteoroids, abandoned spacecraft, instruments humans have deliberately blown up in space, and accidental explosions. One of Crews's solutions is the Hypervelocity Impact Shield — a kind of spacecraft bumper that can stand up to repeated hits from different kinds of objects. The shield is the result of months of experiments conducted by Crews and her partner, scientist Burton G. Cour-Palais, at the Lyndon B. Johnson Space Center in Houston, Texas, where Crews heads the Hypervelocity Impact Research Laboratory (HIRL).

"The danger is the possibility of a collision with a space station or with a delicate and complex instrument, such as a telescope," Crews explains. "If the debris should hit something that was pressurized, it could cause an explosion. Even a tiny particle can put an entire mission in jeopardy.

Basically, the idea is to use not one thick piece of metal on the outside of the spacecraft but layers of thin pieces of material with a certain amount of space in between."

Imagine this: A tiny particle, maybe a piece of rock or metal, is traveling at an extremely high speed. It hits the spacecraft, which is protected by the multiple shields. The impact heats up the particle as it blasts through the first layer of the shield. On the other side, it is no longer one particle but has broken up into a cloud of even tinier particles, called a "debris cloud." These particles are softened because of the heat. When they hit the next layer of the shield, they gain more heat as they make a bigger hole. The debris spreads out more between the layers. This continues until the last debris cloud has gained so much heat that it is more like a liquid or vapor and splats harmlessly against the back plate of the shield.

"The idea of more than one layer is not new," Crews notes. "It was used by the Apollo space mission in the 1960s. Back then, the main worry was about meteoroids hitting spacecraft — there was no man-made junk out there."

What makes the new kind of shield different and more effective is the number of layers, the thinness of the material from which they are made, and the amount of space between them. The HIRL team tried many variations of these factors before finding out what worked best. Experiments continue in the search for an even lighter, more economical, and more easily built shield.

Crews's grandmother had a major influence on her as a child. "She began teaching me to read and do math and algebra when I was four years old. When I was in first grade, if I looked bored, my teacher sent me down the hall to help other children having problems. I don't know how the other kids in my class felt about it, but I loved it. The children I was working with liked it, too. I learned at an early age that you really learn when you have to teach others."

Crews attended the University of Texas and the University of Florida, where she received a B.S. in aerospace engineering. She earned a master's degree in orbital mechanics and astronomy at the University of Houston in 1981.

Crews tells this story about an experience she had as a college student. "It was a test on high-speed aerodynamics, which is a very difficult subject, but I had to have it to get my degree. I hadn't studied. Then I found out that fifty percent of the test score would depend on the way I answered one problem.

"I was under tremendous pressure. I didn't know where to start. I would be humiliated if I got a zero. I was staring at the paper when something weird happened. It was as though a little light bulb shined on the page

*"The danger is the possibility of a collision with a space station or with a delicate and complex instrument, such as a telescope," Crews explains. "If the debris should hit something that was pressurized, it could cause an explosion. Even a tiny particle can put an entire mission in jeopardy."*

. . . . . . . . . . . . . . . . . .

with this formula: $F = M \times A$. Force equals mass times acceleration. You can't get any simpler in physics than that. From that point on, I worked out a derivation [reached a conclusion]. But it did not seem to me that my mind was doing it. It was like a vision. I wrote it down and thought, 'Oh, my goodness.'

"Our teacher was a man whom everyone in class found intimidating, and I was not a person easily intimidated. I was an Air Force brat and had lived in many different places and known many different people. But this man intimidated me. He was so unfriendly! When he returned my paper, he had written on it, 'Excellent. Come see me.' When I went to his office, he asked, 'Where did you get this derivative?'

"I told him, 'I made it up.' He said, 'Would you like to work with me as a graduate student?' At that time, I had only one thing on my mind. I said, 'No, I want to go to work for NASA and be an astronaut.'

"I am still baffled when I think about that vision. Apparently, it was the way part of my mind I don't control responded to the pressure. I didn't totally comprehend what I had done in coming up with an original derivation. Sometimes you don't know what you have. But you should go with the flow when you get it."

## EVE ABRAMS WOOLDRIDGE: ELIMINATING CONTAMINATION IN SPACECRAFT

Eve Abrams Wooldridge grew up in the Maryland suburbs of Washington, D.C., and graduated from the University of Maryland in 1983 with a B.S. in chemical engineering. In 1984, NASA hired her as an engineer at the Goddard Space Flight Center in Greenbelt, Maryland. She studies instrument and spacecraft contamination.

When instruments and spacecraft go into space, they must be clean so that they work properly. Among these instruments are mirrors, lenses, telescopes, windows, and **beam splitters.** One way to test for contamination is to put tape on a surface, pull it off, and study under a microscope anything that came off with it. This procedure must be standardized so that it can be recorded in a "how to" manual. The manual now says, "Put light finger pressure on the tape," but that is not specific enough. The same amount of pressure must be applied to the tape every time. Wooldridge designed a device that measures contamination precisely by keeping a constant amount of pressure on a surface. NASA patented it in 1991.

"When I was younger, I thought engineering was dull and boring — people sitting all day behind a slide rule or a computer," Wooldridge says. "Well, if I had known the opportunities an engineering degree would lead to! I loved math and chemistry, and my father insisted I study engineering

♦ OPPOSITE: On August 15, 1991, an American instrument, the Total Ozone Mapping Spectrometer (TOMS), was put on a Soviet spacecraft and launched on a Soviet rocket. Eve Abrams Wooldridge is shown checking the air cleanliness near the rocket and testing the surface cleanliness of interior rocket surfaces.

**BEAM SPLITTER**
An optical device for splitting a beam of light, sending it in two different directions. It is used for measuring properties of light and testing materials.

to prepare for a good job. As a result, I got a position at the Goddard Space Flight Center, and since then I have traveled to different countries and talked with people all over the world.

"Aerospace engineering is the kind of job where relating to other people is important. Each person is part of the project system. Each person comes to understand the spacecraft in a general way in order to design a system that works for all the areas. To solve a problem, people in the contamination, mechanical, electrical, thermal, and power aspects of the project need to negotiate and compromise.

"There is a definite political aspect to the job. You have to pay close attention to other people in order to know how to approach them when you are presenting an idea you want accepted. You have to be in touch and in tune with both the issues and the people involved.

"What is the difference between a scientist and an engineer? Scientists are more interested in pure theory. They think in terms of what they want to know. Engineers solve problems. Sometimes there is tension between engineers and scientists because engineers are guided by what is practical, what can physically be done.

"There are several women engineers where I work. We have a mix of men and women that provides a balance. In my opinion, women bring an intuitiveness to the work that is valuable."

◆ Margaret Grimaldi is shown working in a laboratory in the Department of Aeronautics and Astronautics at the Massachusetts Institute of Technology in 1993 while on leave from NASA to get her master of science degree.

## MARGARET GRIMALDI: PROVIDING FOR ESCAPE

Margaret Grimaldi, an aerospace engineer at the Lyndon B. Johnson Space Center in Houston, Texas, is one of the inventors of an escape pole, a space crane, and a memory alloy device.

"Work on the escape pole began after the *Challenger* accident [in 1986]," Grimaldi says. "It is designed to allow a crew to escape in case something happens that prevents them from launching into space or from landing on the ground. If they have to let the ship crash, they can escape by means of this pole. It is in a box in the ceiling above where they sit. If they touch a trigger, the pole comes out. They get rid of the hatch and use the pole. Their bodies are connected to the pole, which when ejected points them the right way, under the wing, out of danger." Grimaldi worked on this invention with five coworkers.

"The interesting thing about inventing is that the simplest thing might be the best solution. With the space crane, all the methods were already known and in use. We already had construction cranes on the ground. We had robot arms in space. It was a matter of combining the methods. We thought, 'It seems so obvious; it must have been tried and not worked, because it isn't done.' But then we found that it had not been tried."

The result was the Erectable Manipulator Placement Boom, "a method of building on a space station. It has a robot arm, which can move up and down and manipulate objects. Mounted on the space station, it can reach different positions.

"One of my most exciting projects is the Memory Alloy Retaining Mechanism. I had the original concept and developed it with the help of another NASA engineer, Leslie Hartz. The material is called a memory alloy because the metal 'remembers' how it was shaped at one time. Under certain conditions, it will resume that shape. It has many possible applications in construction, as when areas are not accessible to builders. For example, if they want to fasten something in place but do not have room to put in a nut and bolt, the memory alloy can be inserted. When it remembers its old shape, it becomes a fastener because it cannot be pulled back out again. The metal can be programmed to take on a shape that will in effect make a switch come on, such as turning lights on or off at a certain temperature.

"I have liked airplanes and flying ever since I was a child in St. Paul, Minnesota. My father enjoyed model airplanes. On Friday nights, I would go to the airport and watch the planes land. I knew I wanted to fly planes, so I began early to prepare myself. I kept up my grades in math and science."

Grimaldi majored in aerospace engineering at the University of Minnesota and took part in the Cooperative Education Program there. "Every other semester, I took off from my studies to work at the Johnson Space Center in Houston, in the engineering area. I wanted to be where the action was. The Johnson Space Center is where they train the crews."

After she graduated in 1988 with a bachelor's degree in aerospace engineering and mechanics, NASA hired her to work in the Structures and Mechanics Division at the Johnson Space Center. It was there that she had

> *"The interesting thing about inventing is that the simplest thing might be the best solution."*

worked on the space crane when she was a twenty-year-old student. She still works in the same division, in the area concerned with structures that move.

Grimaldi has a pilot's license and flies a Cessna 172. She may become a flight instructor. "Yes, I want to be an astronaut," she admits. "I guess about all of us do. There is no special program that you can go into for training. Whether you are selected depends on your overall qualifications. Everything I do, I have that in mind.

"When I was in high school, I never dreamed I would work for NASA. But it became a reality for me because I worked hard. When the opportunity came, I was prepared."

## KAREN CASTELL: PROVIDING HIGH VOLTAGE IN SPACE

Karen Castell is an electrical engineer in the Space Power Application Branch of NASA at the Goddard Space Flight Center in Greenbelt, Maryland. She invented the High Voltage Power Supply while working on a spacecraft called the X-Ray Timing Explorer (XTE). The patent was issued to NASA on November 8, 1994. The craft's purpose is to measure the **x-rays** emitted by **black holes** and different star formations. This information will help scientists predict when stars will collapse into black holes and help them evaluate Einstein's theory of gravitational attraction. **High-voltage** power supplies are needed by detectors, which pick up x-rays and **gamma rays.**

"High voltage is critical in space," Castell says. "The problem is how to get high voltage in a way that is safe and will work. Often instruments just stop working because of power failures. The main thing needed is reliability."

Castell's design converts power generated from **solar arrays** and batteries on the spacecraft to high voltage. The invention is now used in the laboratory to supply power. The launching of the XTE spacecraft was scheduled for August 1995.

Castell began working for NASA in 1988. "I'm getting used to it now, but I found it strange at first, being so outnumbered by men in the workplace. It is hard to find female companions. Generally, I am given the same respect as the men I am working with. Occasionally, I meet up with male contractors, usually older, who refuse to take directions from a young woman. This can be a real problem, but there has been plenty of support from my colleagues and supervisors."

Castell, who grew up in the Maryland suburbs of Washington, D.C., took advantage of precollege courses offered at Bethesda Chevy Chase High School. She received a B.S. in engineering from Duke University and

**X-RAYS**
Light is electro-magnetic radiation from an energy source. X-rays, which can go through objects that ordinary light cannot penetrate, come from a very high energy source. They are of extremely short wavelength.

**BLACK HOLE**
Black holes are believed to be collapsed, dense objects many times the mass of our sun. Their gravity is believed to be so powerful that nothing, not even light, can escape its pull.

**HIGH VOLTAGE**
Voltage is the measure of the pressure of the flow of electric current in a conductor. The higher the voltage, the higher the pressure.

**GAMMA RAYS**
Rays of light that come from an even higher energy source than do x-rays and that are of even shorter wavelength.

**SOLAR ARRAY**
A series of panels that converts light into electrical energy.

a master's degree from Northeastern University in Boston, Massachusetts. While in Boston, she also took courses in bioengineering at the Massachusetts Institute of Technology (MIT).

"It was always exciting to think about NASA. I sent in my application, and a supervisor called me up. Although my major field of study, high-frequency magnetics, was not directly applicable to the position at NASA, my research experience as a graduate student was a plus.

"Now I would like to get into an area of engineering that is more

◆ "What I like about engineering is that it is concrete, in the sense that you can see the result of what you are doing," says electrical engineer Karen Castell, inventor of a high-voltage power supply. Here she is in her laboratory at the Goddard Space Flight Center in Greenbelt, Maryland.

humanitarian. One possibility is to design electronics for medical applications.

"I'm also interested in projects that are environmentally oriented. One is the Earth Orbiting System, which collects data on changes in the earth's climate. Another is the ozone-mapping spacecraft. It gives us a map of the ozone layer and shows us where it has been depleted. The ozone layer protects us from harmful ultraviolet radiation from the sun. A proposed project is the Tropical Rainforest Measurement Project. It will look at rain forests, such as the ones in South America, and show us where they have been cut down. Changes in the rain forests affect the climate in all areas of the earth.

"Some people think engineering is not creative, but I find it very creative, especially in the design phase. If a design doesn't work, then you step back and think, 'How else could it be done?' Electrical circuits can be designed in many different ways. There is never one right answer. We're looking for the way that works best to solve our problem.

"What I like about engineering is that it is concrete, in the sense that you can see the result of what you are doing. You see progress. It is very satisfying to have designed something and see it work."

## HATICE CULLINGFORD: RECYCLING ON MARS?

How could humans live on another planet? What about the problems of waste here on earth and in space? To help answer these questions, Hatice Cullingford invented three systems and methods that have been patented by NASA. She did this work while a senior engineer at NASA's Lunar and Mars Exploration Program Office at the Lyndon B. Johnson Space Center in Houston, Texas.

Cullingford's most recent invention, patented in 1993, is the Apparatus and Method for **Cellulose** Processing Using Microwave Pretreatment. As she describes it, "This system converts cellulosic materials such as paper and plant leaves and stalks into sugar, [ethyl] alcohol, or vinegar. The significance of this invention is that we don't have to have large-scale garbage collection, distribution, and landfills. We can solve the garbage problem right at the source — at home, in hospitals, in businesses."

One of Cullingford's previous inventions, patented in 1991, was the Apparatus for Next Generation Life Support Systems. It is a combination of biological, chemical, mechanical, and electrical systems for recycling (or regenerating) air, water, and food — all "life-support consumables." Cullingford says, "The system can be used on Mars or on the moon for long stays. It can be used to enable long stays on earth as well — for example, in Arctic regions, underwater, or underground.

**CELLULOSE**
An important biopolymer that is the primary substance in plant tissue. A component of starch.

"On earth, we have chemical plants with mechanical parts to purify water and waste. The system is huge. The challenge for space is to create a regenerating system that will fit in a spacecraft.

"In thirty years, we might need waste management plants on the moon or on Mars. Almost everything we use there will have to come from earth. We could burn the waste generated there, but I want us to make something else out of it. On a personal level, it is satisfying that I can design for a breakthrough in technology. I like to get results no one has thought of before."

Cullingford was born in Turkey, where she was a chemical engineering student when she immigrated to the United States at the age of twenty. She earned a Ph.D. in chemical engineering at North Carolina State University in 1974.

"When I was a little girl, I wanted to work in the U.S. space program. People in this country don't realize that people all over the world are very concerned with the U.S. space program. When the *Challenger* accident happened [in 1986], people in Turkey were very upset.

"When American astronauts went to the moon, I felt it was a feat for all of us. My family watched a documentary about it and wanted to be part of space exploration.

"My father was not a technical person. He had a liberal arts education. But he thought technology was important for the future. My family has for many generations been education oriented.

"In the fourth grade, in Ankara, Turkey, I started to study biology, physics, chemistry, and math in the public school system. I would come home very excited about what I had learned that day and tell my parents about it. Once my father asked me, 'Why do eggs, which when raw are runny and liquid, become solid when heated? Why do other things that are solid, become liquid when heated?' Ever since that time, I have been trying to understand the most difficult things. Having patents is my way of expressing my uniqueness in this life."

Cullingford lives in Houston, where she is a consultant on projects involving engineering and risk management. She is the founder of Peace University, which promotes world peace through education and technology.

◆ Hatice Cullingford's inventions are aimed at solving the "garbage problem," both here on earth and at future space stations on the moon or Mars.

# ACTIVITIES

# Chapter 4

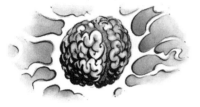

## Project 1

### GROUND CONTROL TO CREW

**Objective**

By acting out a dramatic situation, students can come closer to understanding the excitement and rewards of a career in space. The experience of making important decisions, even in an imaginary situation, helps to build students' confidence in their judgment and thinking abilities.

What could go wrong? What if something does go wrong? In the space program, these questions are constantly being asked. If a problem can be foreseen, it might be prevented or be able to be solved if it does occur.

Acting out possible situations is a way of preparing for them. For practice, reenact the ready-made situation of repairing a sun shield, then create your own emergency situation to act out.

*Repairing a Sun Shield*

As a class, reread the description of the flight mission to repair a damaged sun shield on a satellite in this chapter. Then divide up into two groups. Let most of the class be "ground control." Some students will be in communication with the flight crew, talking to them, encouraging them, asking questions, and giving commands. Some will be monitoring flight information that the crew might not be aware of. Let several other class members be the "flight crew." One person should be captain. Others can be essential personnel, each with special skills. Here are some key phrases to keep in mind as the class creates a dialogue between ground control and the flight crew:

☞ robot arm, damaged sun shield, satellite, mechanical brake, weak arm, monitor, joints, electronic control

Don't forget that in some cases, the crew will be telling ground control what is happening and in others ground control will be giving the crew information. What important piece of information did ground control give the crew in this example?

Now reenact the situation with the dialogue you prepared.

*An Imaginary Mission*

As a class, brainstorm to come up with an imaginary mission to act out. Consider: What is the purpose of space exploration? What might knowledge of other planets teach us about earth? About the universe? About the beginnings of the universe? Why do we want to know about these things? Is there life out there? What is the purpose of a space station? Why would we want to create a space colony? If possible, have a person from NASA come to talk to the class and answer questions about the importance of space exploration. Here are some ideas that might spur your imagination:

☞ A spacecraft has been sent to find out as much as possible about a small body that has been orbiting the earth. The people at NASA do not know what it is or where it came from. They want to get as much information about it as possible, while taking all precautions. The flight crew is permitted to do nothing without the approval of ground control. The crew then loses contact with ground control and is on its own. When communication is restored, what events and discoveries will the crew convey to ground control? What observations will ground control need to communicate to the crew?

Now divide up into groups as in the first exercise, create a dialogue between ground control and the flight crew, and act out this dialogue. If such a situation should actually arise, you would be prepared to deal with it.

**Note to Teacher:** One way to stimulate interest and help prepare for this exercise would be to view videotapes documenting actual NASA missions. One possibility would be the video documenting the *Apollo 13* mission, which had to be aborted because of an explosion in the spacecraft. Bringing the astronauts safely back to earth was an occasion of high drama. See Appendix 3 for video ordering information.

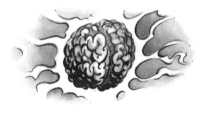

*Project 2*

## THE NAME OF THE GAME

### Objective
Through the entertaining task of creating a board game, students practice working cooperatively and are motivated to learn more about various aspects of space science and exploration.

Follow these directions to create a space exploration board game.

**1.** To help you get started, study your favorite board games to see how they are organized.

**2.** If you're working with a group, talk about real space missions, movies, or books that have inspired you, including science fiction. Work out a general goal or mission for the players.

**3.** What should be on the board? Symbols of the planets, stars, asteroids, galaxies, and so on? What should be in the center? Do you want to use color?

**4.** What should you use to represent the players?

**5.** How many players should there be? Should the players be divided into different types, such as pilots, scientists, and medical experts?

**6.** Is this going to be a game of chance, or will thinking and planning skills be required? Will there be one winner, or will there be various ways for the game to end?

**7.** Think of a catchy name for the game that suggests the skills required to play or some other aspect of the game.

**8.** If you want to take the activity a step further, make a game board and playing pieces and write out the instructions. Then play the game in small groups.

*Puzzle 1*

## GUESS WHO

In this chapter, women inventors at NASA share some events or circumstances of their personal lives. A few of these revelations are listed below. Write in the names of the inventors.

**1.** _____ fell in love with her chemistry instructor.

**2.** _____ immigrated to the United States when she was twenty.

**3.** _____ flies a Cessna 172.

**4.** _____ got in trouble because of her interest in designing.

**5.** _____ found the answer to a quiz in the form of a vision.

**6.** _____ travels all over the world in her job as an aerospace engineer.

**7.** _____ would like to help protect the world's rain forests.

**Answers on page 159.**

# THE RIGHT WORD

*Puzzle 2*

## THE RIGHT WORD

**Across**

**3.** _____ invented a shield that protects spacecraft from damage in collisions with space junk.

**4.** Aboard spacecraft, electricity is made from _____ power.

**6.** _____ discovered a way to make photographs from space clearer.

**9.** The image derived from the process mentioned in the previous clue is called an _____.

**11.** _____ _____ Wooldridge designed a device to put constant pressure on contamination detection tape.

**13.** _____ are people who design and build tools and products to solve specific problems.

**15.** _____ Castell invented a way to produce the high-voltage electricity needed in spacecraft.

**16.** Castell also is interested in developing tools to map the _____ layer.

**17.** Scientists are concerned with _____; engineers are concerned with practical applications of knowledge.

**Down**

**1.** The science of designing and building aircraft and spacecraft is called _____.

**2.** The Hypervelocity Impact Shield is made of several _____ of material.

**5.** High-_____ electricity is needed in spacecraft.

**7.** _____ _____ developed a computer tool to help astronauts identify and fix unexpected malfunctions in their spacecraft.

**8.** Unexpected _____ often occur in space.

**10.** Constant _____ must be applied to contamination detection tape.

**12.** Castell invented a metal that can assume its original shape after being reshaped; it is called a _____ _____.

**13.** The _____ _____ allows flight crew members to exit a spacecraft that is about to crash.

**14.** Margaret _____ invented a space crane to use in building space stations.

**Answers on page 159.**

*Puzzle 3*

## MATCH THE PROBLEM WITH THE SOLUTION

Match each problem that may arise in the space program with
the invention patented by NASA to solve it.

____ **1.** A flight crew reports to ground control that a robot arm being used in a satellite repair mission is malfunctioning. The crew can think of three possible causes, but time is short.

____ **2.** The spacecraft cannot take off until we have a precise measurement of any contamination on its surfaces or on the surfaces of its instruments.

____ **3.** The flight crew has three seconds to get out of the spacecraft before it explodes.

____ **4.** A power failure in space would mean millions of dollars wasted on sending up complex instruments to test theories about black holes and star formation.

____ **5.** To live in space, humans will have to recycle water and waste. This usually requires huge plants. How can we install a purification system in a spacecraft?

**a.** Margaret Grimaldi and five coworkers invented the escape pole to help astronauts exit the ship in case of an emergency.

**b.** Karen Castell invented the High Voltage Power Supply to convert power generated on the spacecraft to high voltage.

**c.** Hatice Cullingford invented the Apparatus for Next Generation Life Support Systems to recycle air, water, and food. She also invented a machine that can be used to convert plant material into sugar, ethyl alcohol, or vinegar.

**d.** Jane Malin invented the Discrete Event Simulation Tool, computer software that design engineers and flight controllers can use to help solve unexpected problems during missions.

**e.** Eve Abrams Wooldridge invented a device for measuring instrument contamination.

**Answers on page 159.**

## Think About It

**Objective**
By comparing then and now, students gain a new perspective on their world and its challenges.

**1.** Christopher Columbus and other explorers in the fifteenth century set out on the ocean for destinations unknown. Their ships and compasses were the best available at the time. Ships could withstand rough seas, travel fast, and go great distances. In what sense were inventors of ships and equipment, who may have stayed at home, also explorers? Does the desire to probe new depths of the ocean and outer space inspire inventors, or do inventions inspire the seekers?

**2.** Barbara Askins is now working as a program manager for a future project, The Assured Crew Return Vehicle. This vehicle will be kept at the future space station. What does the name mean?

What might require the use of such a vehicle? Create four possible scenarios in which the vehicle might have to be used.

**3.** If enough imagination and information go into planning the space station, The Assured Crew Return Vehicle will probably never have to be used. What steps could NASA take to prevent emergencies? How do computers help in looking into the future?

## The Way You See It

**Objective**
Suggestions for writing assignments. Exercises in comparing and analyzing and in using research facilities.

**1.** In space, many things, including human waste, need to be recycled. What kind of recycling systems are being used now in spacecraft? What might be used in a space station? (See the section about Hatice Cullingford.)

☞ For more information, contact the Lyndon B. Johnson Space Center, Information Services, 2101 NASA Road 1, Houston, TX 77058-3696, (713) 483-8693.

**2.** "Shoot for the moon" is a way of saying "Aim for what you really want, even though it may seem out of reach." At one time, the moon was beyond our reach, but then men landed on the moon. What is impossible? Often it is defined as "something that has never happened." How many inventions can you think of that proved the "impossible" was possible?

**3.** Often a breakthrough in technology comes only after years of laboratory and other kinds of work. Find an example of this among the NASA inventors featured in this chapter. Why do you think finding the solution to the problem took so long? What was the inventor doing during all that time?

**4.** After rereading the section about Barbara Askins, tell how she became a NASA inventor and then manager of an important project.

☞ Consider: Was she satisfied with her teaching job? If not, why? What teaching activities led her to the space program? What important steps did she take before asking NASA for a job?

**5.** The inventors in this chapter all do different kinds of work. Review each woman's position and note the different kinds of work she does. Think about the different

jobs you can imagine doing for NASA and explain, in writing, what type of work you would like to do if you worked for the space agency. Why? Be sure to consider your present-day interests.

☞ Does "artificial intelligence" strike a chord with you?

☞ Would you like to teach a robot to talk? Give it personality? What makes you curious?

☞ Do you dream about the adventure of space travel?

☞ Would you like to be at the control board, down on earth, telling the astronauts what to do?

☞ Would you like to find out what happens to a person's body when she or he is in space for a long time?

Take plenty of time to fantasize. ***Shoot for the moon!***

**6.** Science fiction stories are fantasies based on science — stretching the possibilities. Write a science fiction story about the adventures of a woman astronaut. Develop your character by exploring her background and personality. Describe some problems that she must solve.

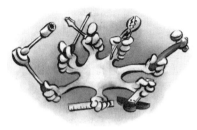

*Imagine That!*

**Objective**
To learn by doing, with cross-curriculum application.

**1. Trouble!** Margaret Grimaldi was one of the inventors of an escape pole designed to help the crew of a spacecraft escape in case of an emergency.

☞ Divide up into teams of three to six students. Let some teams be "troublemakers." Let other teams be "troubleshooters."

☞ Each team of troublemakers should take five minutes to create one or more emergency situations for a spacecraft.

☞ Each team of troubleshooters should then take five minutes to come up with ideas or inventions that would save the crew of the spacecraft and/or the spacecraft itself.

The short time allowed forces creative thinking and stops premature judgment. This exercise can be done several times.

**2. Suited for life.** [Good for individuals or small groups.] Draw or otherwise illustrate a new kind of space suit. Look at pictures of old space suits and new ones. Read descriptions of them.

☞ Information and pictures about early and modern space suits may be available to teachers from NASA's Teacher Resource Laboratory, Goddard Space Flight Center, Code 130.3, Greenbelt, MD 20771, (301) 286-8570.

☞ Consider: What would make you comfortable? Does appearance make a difference? What conditions might you face that would require special equipment in your space suit? Would there be any differences in suits for men and women? What about suits for different gravity conditions? Could there be one suit that fits all?

**3. What's going on up there?** Use the news! Start collecting news articles on the space program. Watch TV documentary or news programs about space. When you have read several articles and/or watched several TV programs, answer these questions:

☞ What are the basic goals of the space program?

☞ What part of the space program seems to cause the most controversy?

☞ In what areas does the program seem most successful?

☞ What have been the major problems?

☞ What programs sound the most interesting?

☞ Would you like to be an astronaut?

**4. Dear Mom and Dad.** Write a letter home from a space station. You have been at the station for three months. What is on your mind? What do you miss about being home? What adventures have you had? How is the food? What do you wish someone would invent to improve life at the space station? These are just a few of the issues you might want to address.

## You Say Yes; I Say No

**Objective**
Topics for debate.

1. We should solve problems here on earth before spending billions of dollars on space exploration. Do you agree or disagree?

2. There is no need to have more space flights with people on board. Machines, including robots, can do all the needed tasks. Do you agree or disagree?

# INVENTING FOR

IS THERE STILL ROOM IN THIS AGE OF HIGH TECHNOLOGY FOR the inventor who is not a superscientist or superengineer? Yes. People with many backgrounds and talents are not satisfied with the way things are. They create new methods and devices that make their home or work life easier and more enjoyable. Their skills come from everyday experiences, from a unique background, or from special education. Often these inventors learn along the way all the steps they must take to convert an idea for something new into a solid reality that they can share with the world — and that can earn them a living.

## HAVING FUN AND LEARNING

What is a game? Often it is a way of teaching or stimulating the mind. It might introduce a new way of looking at things. In some cases, inventions created for entertainment and learning become serious business.

Everyone has heard of Monopoly. Its history goes back to 1924, when Elizabeth Phillips invented a game to teach young people about property and taxes. The Landlord's Game, as she called it, had four railroads, two utilities, a luxury tax space, a place to

♦ The question "What shall we do for a birthday party?" inspired an invention and a business. Children have fun coloring weird images and seeing them magically transformed with a "party fun kit."

# Fun, Profit, and to Meet a Need

park, "Go to jail," and, of course, rental properties. The space where players were paid (the space we call "Go") was called "Mother Earth."

Parker Brothers bought the patent from Phillips and began selling the game in stores. Eleven years later, Charles Darrow obtained a patent on a new version of the game, which he called Monopoly. Parker Brothers dropped The Landlord's Game, and the rest is history.

In 1980, former opera singer Mildred Smith received a patent for a new game called The Family Treedition. Its purpose is to encourage children to study their family history, or genealogy. The game features cards with words such as "brother" and "aunt" printed on one side. It includes pictures and blanks for filling in the names of family members, helping children to build a family tree and understand relationships.

Myrna Hoffman's contribution to children's entertainment also has a long history. Her story shows how an old idea can be a new idea — if it is presented in an original way.

Hoffman started out being fascinated by an old trick done with mirrors. She became obsessed with learning the technique behind it. Then she realized that she was not the only one fascinated by this — it was something that would sell! But getting a patent and bringing the product to market were not easy.

"When I first saw an anamorphoscope, I was captivated," Hoffman says. "I wanted to know more about it. How did it work? Could I do it? I began collecting information on these pictures. Every time I went back to my files, I was fascinated anew. I showed the pictures to people, and they also were excited. But it was fifteen years before I finally set out to learn how to do it myself."

An anamorphoscope is a magical kind of optical instrument. A curved mirror is placed on a picture that has been changed or distorted. The mirror reflects the corrected drawing.

"The secrets of anamorphic art have been eluding people for years," Hoffman says. "Leonardo da Vinci knew them about five hundred years ago. Since then, people have made some modest anamorphoscopes with cylinders, but most of the distortions are not very skillful or creative. No one had done it with a truncated cone, or frustum, before." (A frustum is a cup-shaped cylinder that slopes toward the bottom rather than being straight up and down.)

**OPTICAL PHYSICIST**
A scientist who studies light.

Hoffman had worked as an interior designer, a technical artist, and an art teacher before taking up this new challenge. To learn how to draw distortions for an anamorphoscope, she collected samples of this strange art from around the world. She consulted with **optical physicists,** mathematicians, and computer specialists.

"I was trying a number of things, being thwarted each time. Then it came to me! A ratio popped into my head: 'If this is to that, then this is to . . .' I literally staggered backward. My jaw dropped. It was so easy!

"The following year, we were planning a birthday party for my daughter. I didn't know what to do — we were running out of ideas for how to entertain the children. So we used the anamorphoscope. It was enormously successful! My daughter and the other children loved it. That made me consider marketing it as a product to entertain other kids at parties."

Hoffman created OOZ & OZ, a kit that includes place mats with distorted pictures printed on them and plain cups wrapped with plastic that reflects like a mirror. The surprise comes when you put a cup on a mat and look at it. The curved mirror (plastic) corrects the distortion and reflects a normal picture.

When she began to work on the business and marketing part of her project, she immediately ran into problems. Because the concept is old and therefore already in the public domain, three law firms that specialize in patents pronounced it unpatentable. Fortunately, she found another attorney who was more creative.

"He looked at the novelty of the product, its utility, and the improvement in the existing art that would make it patentable. And he got me a strong patent in only nine months." The patent was issued in 1990.

Hoffman received help in manufacturing and marketing the kit from the Small Business Administration, a federal program, and the Rutgers University School of Management. The Myrna Hoffman Corporation sold many party fun kits and also an activity kit to entertain and amuse children riding in cars or sitting in restaurants or waiting rooms. She has since sold the license to produce, sell, and distribute the products to Pentech International, a large corporation that makes novelty items for children.

## COMBINING CARING AND BUSINESS

People who enjoy helping others are attracted to jobs related to health. Every day, new problems arise in caring for people in hospitals, nursing homes, and private homes. Often caregivers become inventors.

Pediatric nurses (those who work with children) must constantly be concerned about apnea, a disorder that causes youngsters to stop breathing. Premature babies and babies with breathing problems are especially at risk. When a person stops breathing, the loss of oxygen can cause brain damage or death if too much time passes.

Sometimes youngsters stop breathing while they are nursing or drinking from a bottle. Nurse Mary Horn invented a way of letting caregivers know when a baby stops breathing. This device can be affixed to a bottle or pacifier and makes a sound caused by the baby's breathing. The other end is attached to the caregiver's ears. If the sound stops, she or he knows that the baby has stopped breathing. The device also can supply oxygen to the baby.

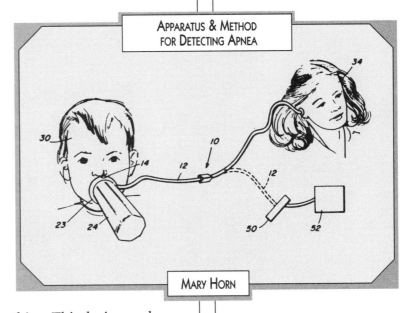

APPARATUS & METHOD FOR DETECTING APNEA

MARY HORN

In 1988, Janine Jagger received a patent for another health care device, a retractable safety needle. The needle is exposed only when in use. This is important because an accidental needle stick can be serious if the needle has been contaminated with the blood of a person suffering from an infectious disease such as AIDS or hepatitis.

Sometimes people find solutions to problems that seem so simple that it does not occur to them that these solutions could be inventions and that they could be patented and sold for a profit. Creating a "simple" solution might, however, require a great deal of effort and an investment of much time and money. The inventor must have faith in the product, enthusiasm, a willingness to learn from others, and, above all, patience.

Lisa Vallino and her mother, Betty Rozier, had all these qualities in creating the I.V. House. Their story is about the process of inventing, manufacturing, and marketing. Their success led to their being invited to

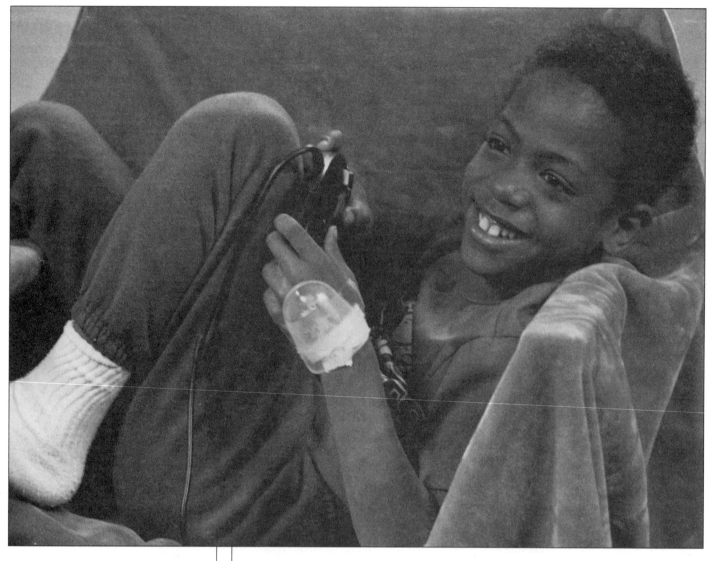

◆ A young home care patient is wearing an I.V. House, the invention of nurse Lisa Vallino and her mother, Betty Rozier.

National Inventors Expo '94, in Washington, D.C., sponsored by the U.S. Patent Office and Intellectual Property Owners, an association of inventors. They received a one-thousand-dollar U.S. savings bond and an award for "Excellence in Creativity" for their invention.

*The Problem*

Vallino, a nurse at Cardinal Glennon Children's Hospital in St. Louis, Missouri, complained to her mother about a constant problem: how to prevent children from injuring themselves by pulling out or accidentally displacing their intravenous (IV) needles. These needles allow liquid food or medicine to enter a patient's veins. The liquid flows from a bag hung above the patient, into a tube, and then through a needle inserted into one of the patient's veins, usually near the top of the hand. The food or medicine enters the patient's bloodstream to nourish or help heal her or him. This method is often used when the patient cannot eat or take medicine via the mouth.

Children in hospitals have a hard time leaving the IV setup alone. They pick at it and pull it loose. Also, if the needle gets bumped accidentally, it can hurt the patient.

To shelter the needle and protect the patient, Vallino and the other nurses spent hours making covers out of clean plastic urine cups, which they cut and taped to the hand. They cut the cups in half and wrapped the cut edges with several layers of tape to try to make them more comfortable where they touched the patient's skin. This took a lot of time; as many as a thousand of these "IV site protectors" are needed each month in a typical children's hospital. For years, Vallino nurtured the idea of mass-producing a protector.

### Taking the First Steps

Vallino knew that her mother was an inventive person who enjoyed working with machinery in her own landscape maintenance and snowplowing businesses. Vallino asked Rozier for help, and Rozier immediately began applying her energy and skills to creating a marketable product. Could they win exclusive rights to the design through the patenting process? Who should make the product? What material should be used? What method?

*Sometimes people find solutions to problems that seem so simple that it does not occur to them that these solutions could be inventions and that they could be patented and sold for a profit.*

"It was my job to handle the business aspects," Rozier says. "These included legal issues such as patents, trademarks, and copyrights. I joined the Inventors Association of St. Louis and listened to other inventors tell how they went through the patenting process. I heard patent lawyers explain about the patenting process. I heard success stories and sad stories about people who had given up on their inventions when they found out they had to prove that there was a market for them. They had not planned to go into business."

Before getting patent protection, an inventor must be concerned about someone stealing her or his idea. Whom can you trust? At one of the Inventors Association meetings, Rozier learned about the Confidential Disclosure Agreement (CDA). "We learned that when we wanted to tell someone about our idea, we could protect its secrecy by just asking them to sign this CDA. We asked potential manufacturers and distributors to sign it also."

Through the Inventors Association, Rozier found a prototype manufacturer — that is, a company that specializes in making original models of new products. "Until you can produce a prototype, all you have is an idea," she says. "Potential buyers insist on seeing a prototype."

The prototype also gives the inventor a chance to see how the product will perform. "We learned about different methods of mass-producing a product and the materials from which our device could be made," Rozier notes. The first method of manufacturing that Rozier and Vallino tried was thermoforming, sometimes called vacuum molding.

### Thermoforming

With this method, the design is stamped out of a piece of plastic using a thermoforming machine. A plastic sheet is put over a mold, and the machine is closed, heated like an oven, and sealed. Then all the air is sucked out, pulling the plastic into the exact shape of the mold. The sheet is removed and the design cut out of the sheet. The cutting process leaves flat edges, or flanges, such as you see in the clear plastic packaging of pens and other objects. The familiar packaging material known as bubble wrap is made with thermoforming.

Vallino and Rozier showed the first prototype to several nurses, who suggested changes such as using a clear plastic that was firm but soft for patients' comfort. The nurses also wanted ventilation holes so that air could pass through the shelter.

"Once we had this prototype, we went to a local patent attorney we had heard speak at an Inventors Association meeting," Rozier says. "She examined the prototype and said it was almost too simple to even apply for a patent. However, several days later she called to say she thought we could apply for a design patent."

Design patents apply to a product's appearance, or design. "The design patent application would at least provide the protection of 'patent pending' status while we continued to develop our ideas," Rozier explains. Patent pending status begins when a patent application is filed and provides secrecy about the device, giving the inventor time to work on refinement and further development. A product may be sold while the patent is pending.

### The Important Search

As part of the process of applying for a patent, an inventor has to make sure there is no existing patent for a similar invention. Inventors sometimes hire researchers to examine patent records for similar technology. Researchers often use computer files located in some public libraries.

"We did our own search to save money," Rozier says. "With the help of a keyword search, the librarian at our local Patent Depository at the St. Louis Public Library provided a long list of related patents. I remember feeling excited, hurrying to carry the heavy books out two at a time, making copies of old patents with pictures and short descriptions, and feeling frantic that someone might have beaten us to it.

"There were hundreds of similar patents! Now that I knew how many others there were, I was scared to tell the attorney. I thought it was all over. I had to tell her, however, because when I signed the application for the design patent, I was obligated under the law to disclose any similar devices discovered while working on ours. Our patent attorney said it was a good sign that there had been so many attempts to make an IV shield. This proved that there was a need for this type of device! The oldest patent I found was dated 1929. Most were complicated gadgets that were never commercially successful.

"Now this was getting exciting! Next we needed to know, Was there a need? Did it solve a problem? Was it marketable? The answers were yes, yes, and yes." The inventors submitted an application for a design patent to the U.S. Patent and Trademark Office in February 1991.

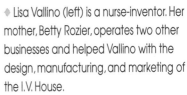
◆ Lisa Vallino (left) is a nurse-inventor. Her mother, Betty Rozier, operates two other businesses and helped Vallino with the design, manufacturing, and marketing of the I.V. House.

Vallino and Rozier chose the name I.V. House for their device. In May 1991, their lawyer sent a letter to the commissioner of patents and trademarks in Washington, D.C., and an application for a federally registered name and trademark. The application told how the device was being used, the exact date when the trademark was first used, and how the mark would be used by applying it to packaging for the device and on the device itself. Having a device or company name with a federally registered trademark adds value to the company and keeps others from using the name. Before a trademark is issued, it is searched through the Patent Office in a manner similar to a patent search.

Meanwhile, Vallino was anxious to sell the device to Cardinal Glennon Children's Hospital so that she would never have to cut up another urine cup. Vallino and Rozier took the first prototype to the materials manager at the hospital. The plan had been to charge fifty cents apiece for them, but when the time came, Rozier could not bring herself to charge this amount for their "simple" product. "I choked when he asked how much the single units cost and said thirty cents. Lisa looked at me with her eyes popping out of her head and calmly finished my sentence with, 'When you buy in quantities of a thousand or more.'"

Vallino presented the I.V. House at a nursing leadership meeting, which included head nurses, clinical nurse specialists, and the vice president of nursing. "They all loved it, and we received our first order for ten thousand units exactly two months later," Rozier says.

"There were problems with our first delivery to the hospital. The units had not been precisely cut during the manufacturing process and were not perfect. We realized that the production method needed to be changed. We also decided to eliminate the flange, or edge, of the unit because we had decided it was hazardous to a child rubbing his eyes."

Luckily, Vallino and Rozier did not have to pay for these imperfect units because of the Uniform Commercial Code. This law gives inventors (or others who provide manufacturing specifications) the right to refuse a newly manufactured product if it does not meet prewritten specifications.

Rozier still thought the device needed more detail in its design. She hired a graphics firm to help improve it. "I just could not charge fifty cents for a product that did not look high-tech," she says. The firm suggested a recessed tape guide with a pattern to make a more professional-looking product without a flange. As a result, Vallino and Rozier found a new manufacturer and used a better, more expensive method of making the device.

### Injection Molding

With injection molding, you can mass-produce items more precisely and make shapes that are not possible with thermoforming. When the product comes out of the injection molding machine, it is ready for packaging. No cutting is required.

With this method, the raw material is thermoplastic pellets or powder, which is poured into a funnel-shaped hopper, or container, where it is heated until it changes into a liquid. This liquid is then injected into a cooled mold and held there under pressure until it returns to the solid state. The mold is in two pieces, a core and a cavity. Tons of pressure hold the two together while the melted pellets or powder takes on the new shape of the mold. Ejector pins strike to knock the finished product out of the mold. The product falls into boxes or onto a conveyer belt, ready for packaging.

"When we were changing the manufacturing method, it was a good time to be sure we had the right material," Rozier says. "I flew to Chicago for an international plastics show, where the different manufacturing processes were explained to me. I was satisfied with our choice of material. We use low-density polyethylene made by the Eastman Tenite company. The material has been preapproved by the Food and Drug Administration for medical purposes."

Rozier took the mold to an engraving company to add a textured tape pattern as a guide for nurses who would secure the needle and cover to patients. "Now we had a product sophisticated enough to apply for the more desirable utility patent status," she says. A utility patent provides more protection against copying than a design patent, which protects only the appearance of a product. A utility patent gives protection against anyone copying the way a device works. On Vallino's thirtieth birthday, July 26, 1991, she and her mother applied for a utility patent to protect the redesigned injection-molded prototype.

*Although Vallino and Rozier made mistakes along the way, none kept them from continuing on with their idea. Even when the mistakes cost money, the inventors looked at them as valuable learning experiences.*

Vallino and Rozier delivered their first order for ten thousand units six months late but in perfect condition. In April 1994, they also began manufacturing a much smaller version of the device to be used for infants. As it turned out, the first child to use this was Vallino's own son, Pete, who was born in December 1993. He had contracted pneumonia and needed to get medicine via an IV.

The patent examiner rejected Vallino and Rozier's patent claims twice. The second rejection was "final." However, the inventors had faith in their product and refused to give up. Eventually, their lawyer persuaded the examiner to consider the unique humanitarian benefits provided by the product, and a patent was granted.

The utility and design patents were issued in 1993. "We changed the 'patent pending' phrase engraved into our mold to 'U.S. Patents 5,167,240 and 335,926,'" Rozier says. The longer number is for the utility patent because many more utility than design patents are issued.

Although Vallino and Rozier made mistakes along the way, none kept them from continuing on with their idea. Even when the mistakes cost money, the inventors looked at them as valuable learning experiences. Their invention is now sold throughout the Midwest to children's hospitals and pediatric units in other hospitals. It is also being used for elderly patients.

"Lisa and I have sold approximately one hundred seventy-five thousand units," Rozier says. "We have attended nursing conferences and made hundreds of phone calls to nurses and purchasing agents. The reaction of Lisa's fellow nurses has ranged from 'Perfect' and 'It's about time' to 'I wish I had thought of that!'"

Vallino and Rozier are ambitious. They want to become wholesale manufacturers, supplying a network of regional distributors. But they also have a more unusual goal. "We would like to find a way to patent and develop the ideas of other nurses in a way that would benefit the nurse-inventor if a device is commercially successful," Rozier says. "There are invention development companies advertising their services. Some of them charge inventors huge sums of money and leave the inventor on her own when it is time to market the product."

They also have other ideas to help nurses. "We will work on a plan to distribute part of our company's profits into nursing scholarships, probably through the American Nursing Association's affiliates in all fifty states," Rozier says. "Not only would nurses get the benefit of a payoff when their product makes money, but a percentage of the product also would help future nurses pay for their education."

According to Rozier, being a woman can sometimes be an advantage in the inventing and marketing business. "I think we are flexible enough to bend with the changes because we are women," she says.

"Lisa and I have learned much. I spread the news of the I.V. House by giving talks on the invention process to students in elementary schools, nursing schools, and college classes on entrepreneurship. It is a good marketing strategy. It is also a chance to give back — to help someone else think, 'If they can do it, maybe we can, too.'"

## FOR MOMS, DADS, AND BABIES

It is not surprising that many inventions by women concern babies. Most are for ordinary situations rather than medical problems or emergencies. The first disposable diaper was patented by Marion Donovan in 1951. Nickie and William Campbell patented the Easy to Hold Baby Bottle in 1986. Later they improved it with a disposable liner. The bottle received the New York Museum of Modern Art's "Design for Better Living" award.

Ann Moore was more concerned with how best to "take the baby along." She borrowed an idea from mothers in Togo, West Africa, and developed it into a product that changed the way Americans carry their babies.

"I was a Peace Corps volunteer in French West Africa when I noticed the inner calm of babies," Moore says. "They were so secure. They were always carried on their mother's back or were being nursed. They were either asleep or alert and curious, looking around them. They rarely cried. I admired the great connection between the African mother and child. We now call it bonding. When I got home and had my own baby, I wanted the same closeness and bonding.

"My mother and I designed the first carrier together. My mother sewed it for my daughter, Mandela. At first we had no thought of marketing it, but many people asked us where they could get one."

The carrier is a soft, padded pouch to hold the baby, with straps that go over the adult's shoulders and around the waist. Moore and her husband, Mike, formed a company to make and market the carrier, called the Snugli. It and similar carriers are now used all over the world.

◆ Ann Moore uses a doll to demonstrate the Snugli baby carrier that she and her mother invented. Moore thought of the design when she was a Peace Corps volunteer and she saw mothers in Togo carrying their children in a similar way.

"They are especially helpful with premature babies who need extra holding," Moore notes. "They allow the nurse to hold the baby while doing other tasks. I was surprised when American women and men began carrying their babies next to the front of the body rather than on the back. It never occurred to me to do it that way, but it is a wonderful idea.

"My best preparation for design work was the fact that my mother taught me to sew. When we first started making baby carriers, many members of my family were making them to help meet the demand."

It took two years for Moore to get a patent for her Snugli design — not

*"If someone from outer space saw examples of human clothing, would they be able to tell how humans move?" That is a question designer Gabriele Knecht likes to ask. Here she is wearing one of her Forward Sleeve designs, which moves naturally with the person wearing it.*

an unusually long wait for a patent. All patents registered at the U.S. Patent Office must be "searched" to make sure that the idea is new and original. The legal work involved in getting a patent can cost three thousand to five thousand dollars, in some cases more.

Moore reminds us, "Having a patent does not give you complete protection. A person could design around the patent and come up with a similar, but different, kind of carrier. However, we were not concerned about that in this case because our main desire was to see more babies carried close to their mothers or fathers."

The Moores sold the Snugli company in 1985. They have formed a new company, called Air Lift, to market other products such as oxygen carriers for people who must be given oxygen constantly.

## WHAT WE WEAR

Since the days of the Emancipation Suit, a nineteenth-century design for comfort, women have been creating new kinds of clothes. Sometimes they succeed in joining high style and practicality.

## A Revolutionary Idea in Pattern Making

"You can hug yourself in the front but not in the back," fashion designer Gabriele Knecht says to illustrate what she means when she talks about the "human element" in designing clothes. Knecht saw (or felt) what no clothes makers ever seemed to notice before — that our arms come out of our sides in a slightly forward direction and we work them in front of the body. In 1984, she received a patent for the Forward Sleeve design based on this observation. The design lets the arms move freely without shifting the whole garment and allows clothes to drape gracefully on the body.

Most clothes patterns have many pieces. Knecht's patterns have only one piece for covering the torso, arms, and legs. To work out a pattern, she begins with a grid, which she cuts out, folds, and combines in various ways. The size can be adjusted by enlarging or reducing the squares of the grid.

Born in Germany in 1938, Knecht came to America when she was ten years old. "In Germany, we never threw anything away," she says. "We unraveled old sweaters and used the yarn to make something else. I can't remember when I didn't sew or knit and crochet."

Knecht studied fashion design at Washington University in St. Louis, Missouri, where she received a bachelor of fine arts degree in 1960. She worked as a designer for several New York companies, creating special lines of children's and adult's sportswear.

Even though she was successful in her career, she did not feel that she was using her full creative potential. She began experimenting and studying early clothing from around the world. "Before there was such a thing as designers, clothes were made by people working together on different tasks," she says. Clothes were cut from material woven on looms of certain widths. This fabric was then cut into triangles, rectangles, and squares to make different garments, using all of the woven fabric without any waste.

Knecht also took courses in physics, cosmology, and other areas of science that seem unrelated to fashion design. The knowledge she gained helped her to understand the shapes she was creating as she worked on her

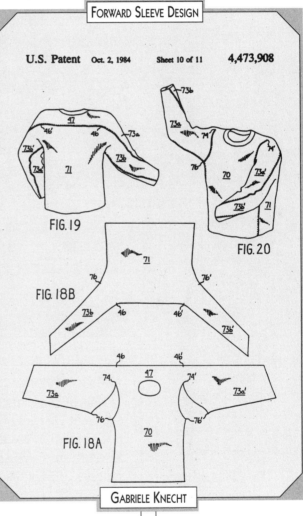

FORWARD SLEEVE DESIGN

U.S. Patent   Oct. 2, 1984   Sheet 10 of 11   4,473,908

FIG. 19

FIG. 20

FIG. 18B

FIG. 18A

GABRIELE KNECHT

♦ Beautiful fabrics and painstaking construction add to the appeal of Gabriele Knecht's designs. Her clothing is sold in fine department stores in New York and around the country. Knecht's Double Helix Spiral Dress in printed silk is shown above.

new method of pattern design. From 1974 to 1984, she filled more than twenty notebooks with sketches. She analyzed all the angles that sleeves can take. She made three hundred experimental patterns and many garments.

Meanwhile, Knecht "freelanced" to support herself, working out of her apartment to design clothing for various manufacturers. In 1982, confident that she had finally created a "new and useful" method of clothing construction, she applied for a patent, which was granted two years later.

At first Knecht was unable to find any manufacturer willing to assist her financially as she started her own business. Her opportunity came when a friend introduced her to a buyer for a Saks Fifth Avenue department store. Buyers are store employees who choose the clothes that will be offered to customers.

The buyer liked Knecht's designs and advanced her the money she needed to create them, exclusively, for the store. Knecht used beautiful fabrics for her designs and was painstaking in her construction. Her clothes sold well. In 1984, the top fashion designers showed their admiration when they awarded her the first annual More Award for the best new designer of women's fashions.

Knecht works in a studio in a large, old building in what is called the Garment District of New York City. The area is home to numerous other design studios and factories that make garments sold all over the world. In Knecht's studio is a huge cutting table, sewing machines, and numerous samples of thread and fabric. "That cutting table is very important to me," she says. "It is where I do everything, including my designing."

Knecht oversees the entire business. This means negotiating contracts with factories to do the sewing, calling people who are in charge of buying clothes for various stores, and making appointments with people who want to see her designs.

A fun part of the job is assigning themes to her collections. For instance, the names of some of the coats in one line are "The Atom," "The

Big Bang," and "The Einstein." Knecht inherited a love of science and its language from her father, who was a physicist.

A special customer of Knecht's is Rachael Worby, conductor of the Wheeling (West Virginia) Symphony Orchestra. Worby used to be bothered by her jacket hiking up when she raised the baton during a performance. Now she wears a special conductor's suit designed by Knecht. In an interview with a Wheeling newspaper reporter after a concert in 1992, Worby said, "My former suit required a shirt, vest and bow tie. The jacket of this one [Knecht's design] buttons to the top and I won't need the extra pieces. The jacket dips in the back and is shorter in front. The trousers are tailored to perfection." Knecht made the two-piece suit from black wool crepe. The jacket has a black satin stitched collar and cuffs and satin-covered buttons. It is lined with black silk.

"The suits I make for women conductors are similar to what male conductors wear — they are tuxedolike," Knecht explains. "They give an image of authority, but it is a feminine kind of authority."

Teaching and lecturing also keep Knecht busy. She shares her ideas about design with students and other groups across the country. She tells people, "There is more to things than we ordinarily see. Being creative is not so much inventing something that didn't exist, but discovering things that are not being used. You have to be able to put yourself in a frame of mind that will allow you to play with ideas. Play is a very important part of it. You need to remember how you played when you were about five years old."

As a child in Germany, Knecht made her own doll clothes and most of her other toys. "I made people, animals, and houses out of seeds, nuts, moss, and fallen branches," she says. "I remember being able to imagine a whole world in a small place." She still likes to work out design ideas in miniature, and she uses tiny mannequins, about twenty inches high, to show examples of her work. She even had a miniature garment rack made for the miniature clothes.

What would Knecht like to tell young people? "If you anticipate results such as making money or becoming famous, you are setting up blocks to creativity. It is nice to be recognized, but if that is your main goal, you may ultimately be disappointed.

"Follow your heart. Work in the field of your choice. Learn as much as

*Knecht makes a point about design with her trademark. When the symbol is turned sideways and separated, you can imagine it as two versions of a person with arms out to the sides. The top view shows the sleeve direction of conventional garments, which are based on a T shape. The bottom view shows the direction of Knecht's sleeves — a forward movement.*

you can in traditional ways, with respect for traditional methods. Then try to look at the task in a new way."

### If You Don't Have the Perfect Figure . . .

Carol Wior is the designer of the Slimsuit, a swimsuit "guaranteed to take an inch or more off the waist or tummy and to look natural." Its main feature is an "inside suit" that helps shape the body. The inside is a natural-looking, tightly woven fabric with an under wire for support of the bust.

Wior was already a successful clothes designer when she imagined a different kind of swimsuit while on vacation in Hawaii in 1986. "I always seemed to be pulling and tugging on my swimsuit, both at the top and bottom, to try to get it to cover me properly," she said. "And I was con-

*Model Nancy Cochran wears her old swimsuit in the picture on the left and her Slimsuit in the one on the right. The secret to a slimmer look is an inner lining that shapes the body.*

stantly holding in my stomach. I sensed that other women felt as uncomfortable as I did. I began to think how I could take this small amount of fabric and make my body look better."

When she returned home, she began experimenting. After nearly two years and a hundred trial patterns, Wior achieved the design she wanted. Her undergarment shapes the body in specific areas, hiding bulges and giving a smooth, firm appearance. Wior sells the suit with a tape measure so customers can make sure the mirror isn't playing tricks.

Other swimsuit designs have included wires and inside suits, but Wior's was different enough to enable her to receive a patent for it. "My inside construction goes all the way around the body, connecting to hidden under wires, so it really does slim and support," she says. "When the woman moves one way, all parts of the swimsuit move with her, even though the inner suit has its own structure."

Wior began designing clothes in 1973 when she was twenty-two years old and living in Arcadia, California. "I was tired of not being able to find a simple, inexpensive dress, especially in black," she explains. Her first studio was her parents' garage. With seventy-seven dollars and three sewing machines, which she bought at an auction, she made dresses she describes as "classic and elegant, but ones a person earning a bank teller's salary could afford." Wior's delivery van was an old milk truck. "I was embarrassed to have buyers see me in it." But the truck did not hurt business. Soon she was selling to major retail stores.

*At age twenty-three, Wior was one of the youngest fashion entrepreneurs in Los Angeles.*

During her first year in business, Wior earned $777,000 in sales. Within three years, she had built a multimillion-dollar business. At age twenty-three, she was one of the youngest fashion entrepreneurs in Los Angeles.

Wior has used creative ideas to make her garments popular, especially with young people. These designs have included underwear, sleepwear, and swimsuits with a tiny computer chip inserted in a corner. If the wearer touched it, she heard a tune such as "Love Me Tender" or "Let Me Call You Sweetheart."

Wior makes different styles of swimsuits in a wide variety of colors and patterns to give the most pleasing effect for the figure. To help sell her designs, she travels all over the country to conduct Slimsuit fashion shows. She also conducts "fit clinics" to help women select the type of suit that is most flattering and comfortable for them.

Wior gives credit to her father, Rolland Weddell, for much of her success. He was a building contractor who invented as a hobby. "My dad was a great inspiration," she says. "Both my parents allowed my brother, my two sisters, and me to do just about anything we wanted as long as it was safe. My parents raised us with a principle — go explore, have fun, but be careful, and we trust you. We grew up with a lot of freedom and a philosophy of 'you can have or do whatever you want in life as long as you work hard and are determined to achieve your goals.'"

## REMEMBER "WOMEN'S WORK"?

Women have traditionally had the main responsibility for keeping homes clean and orderly. Now that so many women work outside the home, that is changing, and men are expected to share the burden. Still, many inventions by women — both past and present — are devices for making housework easier. Often they have been fairly simple — practical ways of doing tasks in less time and with less fuss.

An example of this kind of invention is Dorothy Rodgers's Jonny Mop, patented in 1946 and again, with changes, in 1953. Rodgers (wife of composer Richard Rodgers) hated to clean the toilet bowl and did not like cleaning the scrubber after it had been inside the toilet. Her mop has a handle that holds a disposable swab for swishing around inside a toilet bowl. After cleaning the toilet, the swab is released and flushed away. The patent is no longer in effect, and many other versions of the Jonny Mop are on the market today.

Inventions of this type will always be useful — unless a revolutionary concept in housing catches on. Indeed, if inventor Frances Gabe has her way, fewer people will have to worry about housework. She invented a house that cleans itself.

Gabe (also known as Frances G. Bateson) was granted a patent for Self Cleaning Building Construction in 1984. The U.S. Patent Office had no category for it then because no other patent had ever been issued for such a design. The concept was so unusual that the Inventors Council of Oregon asked her to build a model of the house herself, so that people could see what it was like.

At the time, Gabe was a sixty-nine-year-old builder, artist, and musician who hated housework. She found cheap land outside Newberg, Oregon, that had been used for a dump and cleared it. With the occasional help of a few friends, she built the house she had designed, adding an art studio for herself. She has lived in the house happily ever since, and the land is now covered with trees.

Gabe chose cinder block, painted a soft white, for the outside construction because it is termite-proof and inexpensive. Inside are sixty different laborsaving devices. "I can open a valve, push a button, and leave. When I

**Frances Gabe's self-cleaning house has sixty different laborsaving devices, including a dishwasher that doubles as a cabinet.**

come back, the house is clean," Gabe says.

Each room has a device in the ceiling to supply a fine spray of water or mist with enough force to clean a room. Electric timers allow one room to be cleaned at a time. Water and detergent can be applied first, followed by a rinse of water alone. Blowers help air-dry the rooms. Floors slant toward drains. Walls are coated with a resin, a liquid that when dry is waterproof. Furniture is made from a composition material that is waterproof. "It is soft and attractive and can be made in different colors and patterns," Gabe says.

In the kitchen is a cupboard that is also a dishwasher — no need to

*Women are at the doorstep of
becoming equal partners in the creative arts
and sciences. This cannot happen too soon — their contributions
are important to meet the needs of our changing world. This does
not mean that all women will, or should, become engineers or
entrepreneurs. They should, however, have the choice.*

remove the dishes after washing! In the bathroom is a heated bathtub and a dry toilet. The toilet uses paper liners that are automatically put in place and disposed of.

What does the inventor like most about the house? "I enjoy the windows," she says. "They are not just holes in the wall. They let me see the forest." The windows are long expanses of glass built into the walls. Flush with the walls both inside and out, they are easy to clean. The space between the inside and outside glass provides insulation. Special devices make them easy to open and close.

Gabe's house attracts so many visitors that she has had to discourage them by charging five dollars per person for a tour. "It's my home," she explains.

Born in 1915, Gabe learned the building trades by working with her father, Fred Arnholtz, an Oregon-based architect-builder. "From the time I was two years old, he took me with him to construction sites," she says. "He built houses and big buildings all over the country."

Working with her father and his employees, Gabe learned plumbing, carpentry, electrical work, and other aspects of building. However, her teenage years were troubled. She did not get along with her stepmother, and she left home to live with another family, doing housework for her room and board while she attended school. When she was fourteen, she entered the Girls' Polytechnic College in Portland, Oregon, finishing a four-year program in two years.

Gabe married an electrical engineer, and when her husband could not find work, she formed the Bateys Building Repair business to employ them both. She operated the business for forty-five years. "I would buy a house in bad condition, fix it up real nice, and sell it," she says.

Many people who for one reason or another cannot perform household tasks have shown an interest in Gabe's self-cleaning house. "I have had many elderly people say to me, 'Oh, this is just what I need, because I can't do that work anymore,'" Gabe says. "Also, handicapped people think it's wonderful because all they have to do to clean is push a button. The house would be perfect for a group home. It would be ideal for couples who work outside the home."

Universities, builders, promoters, inventors, architects, and contractors also are interested in Gabe's design. "I will be glad to sell the rights," Gabe says. "There are other things I want to do." Among those things are painting, sculpture, and ceramic work, for which she is noted in Oregon, and playing the piano, violin, and mandolin.

## WHY IS IT IMPORTANT THAT WOMEN INVENT?

Rosalyn Yalow, trained as a chemist, works in the medical field. As she accepted the Nobel Prize for medicine in 1977, she said about women, "We must believe in ourselves or no one else will believe in us."

Women are at the doorstep of becoming equal partners in the creative arts and sciences. This cannot happen too soon — their contributions are important to meet the needs of our changing world. This does not mean that all women will, or should, become engineers or entrepreneurs. They should, however, have the choice.

The proportion of women who have been granted U.S. patents is relatively small (only about eight percent in 1993). Yet women do invent — although the credit often has gone to their fathers, brothers, and husbands, especially in the past. As we have seen in this book, when women are trained as scientists and their environment becomes the 3M Company, DuPont, or NASA, their contributions are impressive.

Throughout the history of Western civilization, we have lost almost half of humanity's potential inventors. Economic growth depends on new ideas, new products, and new social inventions. We should not waste half our potential. There is no evidence that women will invent differently, but they can be more active participants in the patenting process. We can double our options by doubling the number of ideas from which to choose. As Rosalyn Yalow has said, "The world cannot afford the loss of the talents of half of its people if we are to solve the many problems which beset us."

# ACTIVITIES

## *Project 1*

### A SUCCESS STORY

**Objective**
By creating pictures and dialogue to retell the story of the Vallino/Rozier invention, students will gain a clearer understanding of the process of inventing, obtaining a patent, manufacturing, and marketing.

You may do this activity as a group, letting one person be the artist, or each student may do her or his own drawings.

☞ Reread the section about Lisa Vallino and her mother, Betty Rozier. Create a comic book–style story about them and their enterprise. It does not have to be funny, although some humor might make it more interesting. Give the story a jazzy title.

☞ Show, with pictures, the steps the two women had to take before they could say, "At last, we're in business!" For instance, you might begin with a drawing of a group of grumpy nurses holding scissors and saying, "We spend far too much time cutting up urine cups to make IV covers!" You may illustrate the steps fully if you wish or use simple symbols or cartoon pictures.

☞ Hint: Jot down each step mentioned in the text, no matter when it happened. You should have many different steps when you are through. Then put them in order. You might group together events that seem to have happened at the same time.

Sometimes the two inventors had to work on different aspects of the project or on several things at once. You can use the flashback technique, saying, "While Lisa was doing (whatever), her mother was doing (whatever)." Don't forget to incorporate their mistakes or setbacks, for dramatic appeal.

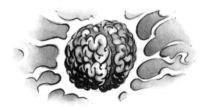

## *Project 2*

### MAKE IT BETTER

**Objective**
To help students look with new eyes at common objects and tools around them

Too often we say, "It's no use; this idea won't work," when we really mean, "This tool is not designed to allow me to use it the way I would like." Think creatively when using old, everyday objects. If the tools are too limited in what they can do for you, imagine how you might change them!

**1.** Choose an object in the classroom and invent an improvement of it. For instance, you might invent a new kind of globe. How could it be different? (Maybe a computer connection makes a country light up when it is mentioned. Use your imagination!) List several things a new globe might do or how it might look. Let your ideas serve some purpose. Don't worry about whether they are possible or whether you will actually be able to create the new globe.

**2.** After looking at trademarks and logos (symbols) for products or companies mentioned in this chapter, create a name for your new invention. It should be different from any other name, tell something about the product, and be easy to say and remember.

**3.** Design a logo for your invention. This is a visual symbol that can be used with the name or by itself. Perhaps you can turn the name of your product into a logo (like the Coca-Cola symbol). Consider: Is it simple? Easy to remember? Attractive? Remember, you can use words, pictures, and symbols.

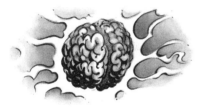

*Project 3*

# THE INVENTING GAME

### Objective

By following the account of how Monopoly came to be, students will see that there is often no single "inventor" for a "new" product. Ideas evolve! Students can then create their own version of the board game, taking inspiration from The Landlord's Game/Monopoly but bringing in the modern world of business and their own lives.

All games were invented by one person or a group of persons. In time, others came along and changed the game. Such changes can be called improvements. What would you call the changes if you thought they had spoiled the game?

When someone invents a new game, she or he does it to solve a problem: How can I spend my time on this rainy day? How can I have more fun this afternoon? How can I entertain this little kid I have to baby-sit? How can I make this game more fun?

One popular game is Monopoly. Who invented Monopoly? You can find out if you look at a Monopoly board. Printed in the center is the following:

Registered in U.S. Patent Office
Copyrights 1935, 1946 by Parker Brothers, Inc.
U.S. Patent 2,026,082

At right is a copy of the cover of this patent document. Does the picture bring back memories of buying, selling, trading, and "Go to jail"? The cover sheet tells us (at the bottom of the page) that Charles B. Darrow was the inventor. At the top of the page, we see that the patent has seven pages of pic-

tures. (The pages with words come later.)

We're looking at the first picture page. We learn that Darrow applied (filed) for the patent on August 31, 1935, and that the patent was granted four months later. We can draw some conclusions from this information. We know that Monopoly has been around quite a while. We also know that Darrow invented Monopoly. But *was* he the inventor?

In an old version of Monopoly, the board has two patent numbers. One is the number listed above; the other is patent number 1,509,312. On the next page is a picture from the earlier patent. Note that it is called The Landlord's Game.

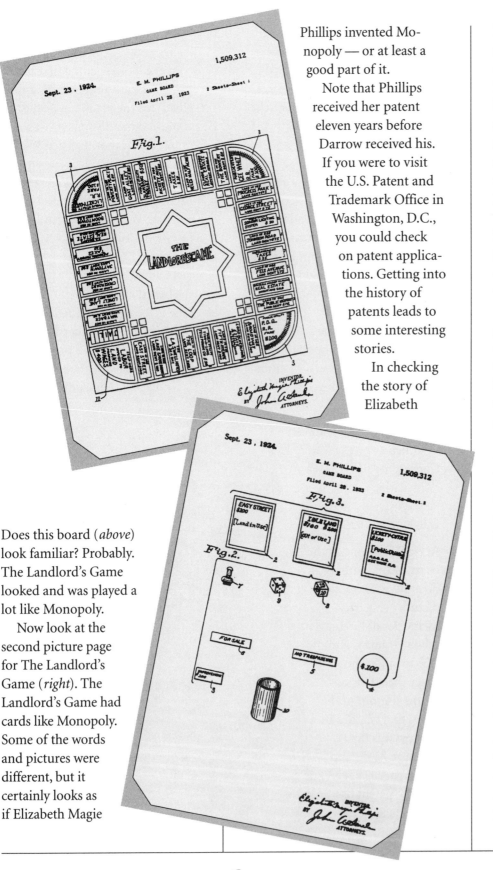

Phillips invented Monopoly — or at least a good part of it.

Note that Phillips received her patent eleven years before Darrow received his. If you were to visit the U.S. Patent and Trademark Office in Washington, D.C., you could check on patent applications. Getting into the history of patents leads to some interesting stories.

In checking the story of Elizabeth

Does this board (*above*) look familiar? Probably. The Landlord's Game looked and was played a lot like Monopoly.

Now look at the second picture page for The Landlord's Game (*right*). The Landlord's Game had cards like Monopoly. Some of the words and pictures were different, but it certainly looks as if Elizabeth Magie

Phillips, we discover that she received another patent in 1904 — twenty years earlier. We see that Lizzie Magie invented an even earlier version of Monopoly. And we see that by 1924, she used the name Elizabeth rather than Lizzie and that she had married and taken her husband's name, Phillips.

Now look at the 1904 game board (*opposite*). Look really closely. The space where one was paid — the one we now call "Go" — was called "Mother Earth."

Lizzie Magie manufactured the game herself and sold it where she could. Later it was used in schools to teach economics. The inventor had wanted to use her game to teach about property and taxes. She did a pretty good job.

Parker Brothers, the company that sells Monopoly, bought Phillips's patents. In the first version of Darrow's Monopoly, the company gave her credit for the invention by printing her patent number on the board. By investigating Monopoly's patent, we have learned a good deal about inventing. We also have learned that this game was developed by a woman, who may have been the first person to make a game out of economics.

Like any good invention, The Landlord's Game/Monopoly has been changed by others who have adapted the rules to their own tastes. Do you ever add to or change the rules when you play Monopoly? If so, you, too, are an inventor.

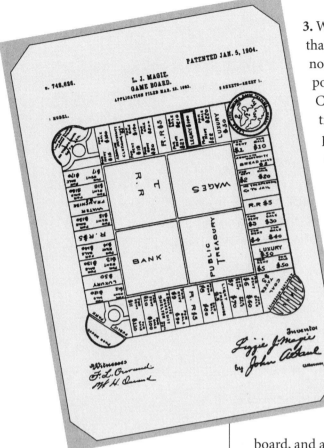

**Puzzle 1**

## WORD SCRAMBLE

Unscramble the missing word in each of the following sentences.

**1.** Ann Moore was a Peace Corps volunteer in the African country of _____ when she saw an atypical way of toting babies. **goto**

**2.** Myrna Hoffman was _____ with anamorphoscopes, so she learned how to make one. **niscafated**

**3.** Lisa Vallino concocted the I.V. House because she was tired of making sheaths for IV needles out of _____ urine cups. **caplist**

**4.** Gabriele Knecht noticed how people's arms work and contrived a new kind of _____ construction. **velees**

**Answers on page 159.**

**3.** What social problems that are connected to economic problems might be pointed up in the game? Consider: pollution; traffic congestion; both parents working outside the home. List others.

**4.** What are some alternatives to jail for wrongdoers? Example: "Go clean up the trout stream." What are some possible punishments for violating the rules of the game? Example: You could put a red light on the board, and a player would lose her or his driver's license if she or he went through it too many times.

**5.** What messages or commands that reflect the hazards of modern life could you put in the squares on which players might land? Examples: "You're fired"; "Train for a new job"; "Buy a computer."

**6.** How might you use credit cards in addition to money?

☞ Use your lists to help you design a new version of the game. If you have trouble fitting your ideas into the game as it now exists, remember that you are the inventor. Make it work!

☞ Darrow's board has properties named after streets in Atlantic City, New Jersey, a place he loved to visit. If you were to redesign Monopoly, would you name the properties after places in your town? How about naming the properties after your friends or relatives — Uncle Joe's Telephone Company or Sandra's Art Shop?

☞ Following are some other things to think about:

**1.** What would you call your game?

**2.** What kinds of businesses would show up on the board that were not in existence when Monopoly was created? List seven new businesses.

*Puzzle 2*

## QUESTIONS AND ANSWERS

Match the questions that inventors in this chapter asked themselves
with the inventions that resulted from those questions.

___ **1.** Can something so simple receive a patent?

___ **2.** What will children do with it?

___ **3.** Why are these babies so peaceful?

___ **4.** How do people move?

___ **5.** How do most women want to look when
they are at the beach?

___ **6.** What if you never had to put dishes away
after washing them?

**a.** Forward Sleeve (Knecht)

**b.** Snugli (Moore)

**c.** OOZ & OZ (Hoffman)

**d.** I.V. House (Vallino and Rozier)

**e.** Slimsuit (Wior)

**f.** Self Cleaning Building Construction (Gabe)

**Answers on page 159.**

*Puzzle 3*

## AN ANAMORPHO *WHAT*?

**Across**

**1.** Hoffman's anamorphoscope toy
is based on a _____.

**4.** Inventors must make sure there
are no _____ patents for
their design or method.

**7.** When parents hold a baby close,
this aids in the _____ of
baby and parents.

**8.** For your next party, get a party
fun _____.

**10.** _____ invented a device
to warn caregivers when a baby
stops breathing.

**11.** A Confidential _____
Agreement protects an inventor

when she discusses her idea with
others.

**12.** An _____ is a curved
mirror that makes a distorted picture look normal.

**15.** _____ coinvented the I.V.
House.

**18.** A retractable _____
_____ protects health care
workers from accidental needle
sticks.

**19.** The idea for the Snugli baby
carrier originated in _____.

**20.** Knecht says inventors need to know how to _____.

**23.** Knecht invented a new design for the _____ of a garment.

**24.** _____ has designed jackets for orchestra conductors.

**Down**

**2.** _____ is a process used to make bubble wrap and other plastic products.

**3.** Nurses and others who care for infants and young children are concerned about _____.

**5.** Did your mother carry you in a _____ when you were a baby?

**6.** _____ invented a needle that prevents accidental sticks.

**9.** The _____ was invented by a mother-daughter team.

**13.** _____ got the idea for her invention while in the Peace Corps in Africa.

**14.** _____ invented a party game called OOZ & OZ.

**16.** A _____ is a model of a proposed invention.

**17.** A _____ patent provides

AN ANA-MORPHO WHAT?

more protection than a design patent.

**21.** _____ Vallino coinvented the I.V. House.

**22.** _____ was the first infant to use the special small I.V. House.

**Answers on page 159.**

*Think About It*

**Objective**
By making comparisons, students can relate aspects of inventing to their own lives and learn the value of seeing in a new way.

**1.** Ann Moore didn't get her idea for a new kind of baby carrier until she had a baby. She remembered her stay in Africa and the mothers she met there. Travel gives us a new perspective. Moore borrowed an idea from African women and adapted it for American parents' needs. Have you seen or heard of other foreign customs or devices that could lead to new products for people in the United States? Consider: How do people in different countries cook and eat? What kinds of shelter do they have? What vehicles do they use for transportation? How do people amuse themselves or compete in sports? If you are foreign born, what are some things you miss from your native land? Could you adapt some game or way of cooking to the United States?

**2.** Why do you think trademarks are important? (See the discussion of trademarks in Appendix 1.) What does the name of a product have to do with how it is sold? Review the trademarks used by the inventors in this chapter. Look at your clothes, your room, and items in and on your desk. Note how many products are known by a special name given by the manufacturer. Some trademarks have become so well established that we ask for an item by that name rather than its "generic" name (for example, Kleenex instead of facial tissue). How many examples can you think of?

**3.** When Myrna Hoffman applied for a patent for her anamorphoscope activity for children, lawyers in three firms that specialize in patents told her "no way" because the technology is in the public domain and cannot be patented. What do you think is the meaning of the phrase "in the public domain"? After brainstorming definitions, check the official definition in a dictionary. How close did you come?

What other items that don't involve inventions or technology are said to be in the public domain? There are time limits on patents. How do legal rights change when a patent is no longer in effect? Copyright laws protect the rights of authors to exclusive use of their own writings or music. When the copyright for a book expires, how does that change the public's right to use that book?

**4.** Myrna Hoffman eventually found a more "creative" patent lawyer who saw her anamorphoscope differently. The lawyer saw that although the basic technology was old, Hoffman's methods and application (her way of using the technique) were new.

Let's look at an extremely important invention — the wheel. It is old technology in the public domain. But how many inventions use it? Look around your room, home, and school. List all the things you see that use some version of the wheel. In each case, tell what the wheel does, what task it helps to perform. What does this exercise tell you about the creative mind?

**5.** Who invented the screwdriver? The fork? Chopsticks? The pencil? We use a number of very basic devices every day. What are some other basic machines, devices, and methods that we use in countless ways? List them and discuss the scientific principle behind each one.

**6.** Frances Gabe wanted to "improve living conditions" through her inventions. To her, this meant less housework for women. How would you like to improve living conditions in the world? What would you like to invent to make your school a better place? Your home? Your community?

**7.** Clothing designer Gabriele Knecht says that playing is an important activity for inventors. What do you think she means by that? Discuss all the different things that are going on when a child of about five is playing by herself or himself or with others. How can play help a young person or an adult come up with new ideas?

## *The Way You See It*

### Objective
Suggestions for writing assignments. Exercises in comparing and analyzing and in using research facilities.

**1.** Nurses often come up with new ideas for their patients' comfort or to help them in their work. If you have been in a hospital, what conditions did you find irritating or uncomfortable that might be improved through creativity? Some things you might consider are how the sun comes through the windows, the location of the buzzer used to call for assistance, and the way the bed is adjusted.

**2.** What do patent lawyers do? Why are they necessary? Why can't a person just fill out the patent application and wait for the patent to be granted or turned down?

**3.** Let's say that Patricia and Paul claim to have invented the same thing — perhaps a machine that will write a musical note on a staff when it is played. What kinds of proof would Patricia or Paul need to prove that she or he was the first person to come up with the idea? What kinds of records should an

inventor keep if she or he plans to apply for a patent?

**4.** Through the ages, people in different cultures, living in different climates, have found different ways to carry their babies. What are some of these devices and methods? Which ones do you like and think you might adapt?

**5.** List some professions or jobs that women and men do. What problems in the workplace would result if a woman or man had to bring her or his child to work? Can you think of ways to help modern women and men in offices, laboratories, and other work settings be able to have their children close by? How could inventions or technology help? Dream up some ideas! They might be the wave of the future.

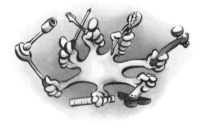

## *Imagine That!*

### Objective
To learn by doing, with cross-curriculum application.

**1. A cloak of invisibility?** Carol Wior designed a bathing suit that makes people look slimmer. Gabriele Knecht designed a kind of sleeve that allows more freedom of movement. What are your pet peeves with clothing? Follow these steps to develop some ideas to fix the problems.

 As a class, brainstorm a list of clothing problems.

 Choose one or two problems from the list. Brainstorm ideas to fix these problems.

 Choose a solution that seems possible to invent and use.

 Go through a mock patent application process. (Sample forms are included in Appendix 1.) Try to find out whether your idea has already been patented. Keep in mind that many patents are simply changes to, or improvements of, an existing design.

 Go through a mock trademark application process. (Sample forms are included in Appendix 1.) What would you call your invention? How would you display the name? Draw a logo. Try to find out whether your idea has already been trademarked.

**2. Shades of Rube Goldberg.** Goldberg was a newspaperman famous for his cartoons of unusual contraptions created for humor. He used numerous mechanical devices — bells, whistles, pulleys, cranks, levers, and wheels. Each contraption performed a simple task such as opening a birdcage, giving a haircut, walking a dog on a treadmill, or turning on a fan. The task

was done through a series of steps that were often impractical but all based on scientific principles. They might have been crazy, but they worked!

You can do a Rube Goldberg project. Gather together unrelated objects such as a book, a bottle, a ruler, a pair of scissors, paper clips, bandages, an iron, a toothbrush, a skateboard, a clothespin, and so on. Create a mechanical device out of them. Have it perform some task. It doesn't have to be practical; it just has to work!

**3. When a mousetrap is more than a mousetrap.** One group of high school students used a mousetrap to make a catapult to hurl jellybeans. Others used the same mousetrap to make vehicles. Experiment with mousetraps. See if you can come up with similar or different uses for a mousetrap.

Now pick another product that has a clear function and mechanical parts. By identifying all the parts and the principles that make it work, use it for three other functions.

**4. If I could change that …** Challenged to invent something to make her own life easier, a high school girl tackled a recurring problem in her home. She invented a toilet bowl alarm that makes a loud noise when the toilet seat is left up. Make a list of three chores you dislike or dread or three things you would like to change. For each one, think of an invention that would ease the burden. Describe

how these inventions would work. Let your imagination run wild!

**5. The name of the game.** [A group or individual project.] Create a board game with a central theme of inventing and getting a patent. Use drawings, symbols, and words. The board design might be in the form of a maze, with some paths that lead nowhere. There may be times when the seeker has to "Go back to square one" or is penalized or fined. There may be battles between people with the same idea. For the inventive person with a good imagination, the possibilities are endless. You might patent the game and become rich!

**6. Special resources.** In Appendix 1, you will find an address to which you can write for a list of the patent depositories in the United States. Patent depositories have all U.S. patents on microfilm. Each depository has at least one librarian trained by the U.S. Patent and Trademark Office to help you use the services. If possible, visit your local patent depository. Learn how patents are placed into categories called classifications. What is the classification number for puppets? What is the classification for internal combustion engines? What is the classification for one of the inventions that you've created?

**7. Filing for a patent.** [A group activity.] If you had an invention that seemed unique, how would you file for a patent? Take an invention and go through a mock patent application process.

☞ As a class, select students to represent various people in the process. For example, there should be at least one patent attorney, a patent examiner, and an inventor. There might be another inventor who claims that she or he is the true creator of the idea. You may need a researcher to do a patent search, an artist to make technical drawings, and a craftsperson to build a model.

☞ Prepare arguments to show that your invention is new, useful, possible, and your own idea. If you have access to a patent depository, do a patent search to determine whether anyone else has thought of the idea before.

☞ If possible, the teacher could invite a patent attorney to class to help with this project. Sample patent application forms are included in Appendix 1.

☞ Dramatize the process, with each student playing her or his assigned role. Perhaps a separate group of students could create the dramatization.

**8. To market, to market.**

☞ Pick one of the inventions you have created. What would you have to do to market your invention? How many people would be likely to buy it? Check with people you know and merchants in your community.

☞ Think about how you might manufacture your product in quantity (mass-produce it). Check costs of materials, labor, and machinery. What else would cost money? Would shipping be a major cost?

☞ Where would you advertise? How would you appeal to your special audience? How much would advertising cost?

☞ Where would you sell your product? In a store? A catalog? Door to door? What would be the cost of selling the product?

☞ How could you design your product so that it would be more attractive? What color would you choose? What shape? What logo, or symbol, would you use?

**9. On Broadway.** Form small groups to create scenes for a musical comedy about women inventors, using the women mentioned in this chapter. When you are familiar with an inventor, work on music and lyrics. Make up songs with original tunes or put your own words to tunes you know. Or take existing songs and change them a little, adding the name and accomplishments of the inventor. Add dance steps to the songs. Each group can then perform its skit as part of the show for another class.

## You Say Yes; I Say No

**Objective**
Topics for debate.

**1.** A person who does not have a scientific education has little chance of becoming an inventor in this age of high technology. Do you agree or disagree?

**2.** Is it fair for one person or company to have exclusive rights to make and profit from an invention that is important to everyone's well-being?

*1*

# PROTECTING

ON APRIL 10, 1790, PRESIDENT GEORGE Washington signed a bill that read in part, "Congress shall have power ... to promote the progress of science and useful arts by securing for limited times to authors and inventors the exclusive rights to their respective writings and discoveries." Thus began the U.S. patent system.

What is a patent, and why do we need it? A patent is a legal document that helps both inventors and the public. It gives an inventor control over the use of an invention that may have taken years and much money to develop. It also makes the new technology available to the public.

Since 1790, the patent law has been revised several times, but its purpose is still the same: to encourage inventiveness in society. Today inventions are distinguished from writings, which are protected by copyright laws, not patents.

An invention, according to U.S. patent law, is something that is "novel, non obvious, and useful." You do not have to apply for and receive a patent to manufacture and sell an invention, but if you do not have a patent, someone could legally "steal" your idea. If you do have a patent, you can sue anyone who might try that.

If an inventor manufactures and sells an invention without applying for a patent, she or he might not be able to get a patent. If the inventor describes the invention in a publication, she or he must apply for a patent within a year of publication.

If you want to learn more about an invention, you can find a description in a patent filed at the U.S. Patent and Trademark Office in Arlington, Virginia. Or you may visit any of several U.S. Patent and Trademark Depository Libraries, which are located throughout the country.

# And Sharing a New Idea

For a complete list of patent libraries, contact the U.S. Patent and Trademark Office, Crystal Plaza 3, Room 2CO4, Washington, DC 20231, (703) 308-3924. Each patent depository has most U.S. patents on microfilm. Other helpful books and electronic search facilities also are available. Each depository has at least one specially trained librarian who can help with a patent search.

When the Patent and Trademark Office grants a patent, it is given a classification number based on the type of invention. For instance, a board game would have a different classification number than an internal combustion engine. This makes it easier to search for patents. Each patent also is assigned a sequential number that is one digit higher than the number assigned the previous patent. In this way, we know which patent came first without having to check the date.

Patents are not listed by the gender of the inventor. However, it is possible to do a name search (by computer for recent patents). By looking at the full names of inventors, you can get an approximate count of the number of women who have received patents and see what they invented. The Patent and Trademark Office has done this kind of survey a few times over the years.

*A patent is a legal document that helps both inventors and the public. It gives an inventor control over the use of an invention that may have taken years and much money to develop. It also makes the new technology available to the public.*

Since the patent system was established in 1790, more than two hundred thousand patents have been granted to women who were U.S. residents. In 1993, approximately eight percent of patents granted to U.S. residents included the name of a woman, with more in the field of chemistry than in any other field. This percentage is much higher than in the past, but obviously women still have a long way to go.

Proving that an invention is "new, non obvious, and useful" can be quite a job. The inventor must provide the Patent and Trademark Office with convincing evidence that her or his idea will work. The application must include a written description of how to make and use the device. In some cases, samples may be provided. For a design or mechanical device, drawings may be helpful. If the invention is found to be truly new (even though based on old technology) and if it has a useful application, the inventor is granted a patent.

The basic fee for filing a patent application ranges from $150 to $730. Lower fees are charged applicants who are "small entities" — for example, an independent inventor, a small business, or a nonprofit organization. Strict regulations govern the patent application process. Most inventors hire a lawyer to help them. Patent examiners often turn down ideas or require several revisions before issuing a patent.

♦ Rose O'Neill poses with her popular Kewpie dolls, for which she obtained a design patent. This made it illegal for anyone to try to make and sell a doll that looked like a Kewpie without her permission.

## KINDS OF PATENTS

Because there are different kinds of inventions, there are different kinds of patents. A *utility patent* is granted to "new, useful and not obvious processes, machines, compositions of matter and articles of manufacture." This type of patent is most often granted for an improvement on an existing method of performing some task. Medical patents, such as those issued for Gertrude Elion's new drugs (see Chapter 3), come under this category. The Snugli baby carrier, invented by Ann Moore (see Chapter 5), also received a utility patent. Utility patents are good for twenty years.

A *design patent* is for a new, original ornamental design for an article of manufacture. "Ornamental" means that the patent covers the way the article looks rather than how it works. Rose O'Neill, an illustrator of stories and advertisements, was granted a design patent for the Kewpie doll, which became very popular. Ann Moore also received a design patent for the way her baby carrier looked. Design patents are in effect for fourteen years.

A *plant patent* is for plants that have been reproduced by means other than seeds, such as by rooting of cuttings or by grafting. Cecilia (Dee) Bennett was granted a plant patent in 1986 for her Miniature Rose Plant.

## TRADEMARKS AND TRADE SECRETS

Instead of (or in addition to) a patent, an inventor may apply for trademark protection. A trademark is a brand name or symbol (picture or drawing) used to identify a person's or a business's products. For instance, DuPont gave a special name, Kevlar, to the new fiber that Stephanie Kwolek helped create (see Chapter 3). The 3M Company uses the name Scotchgard for its fabric protection product, invented by Patsy Sherman and other 3M chemists (see Chapter 3).

To keep others from using a trademark, an inventor (or business) can register the name with the U.S. Patent and Trademark Office. Many trademark owners use a symbol such as ® or ™ beside the product's name to show that they expect the exclusive right to use this name. ® can be used only if the trademark is registered with the Patent and Trademark Office. ™ is used to show that all rights to that trademark are being claimed.

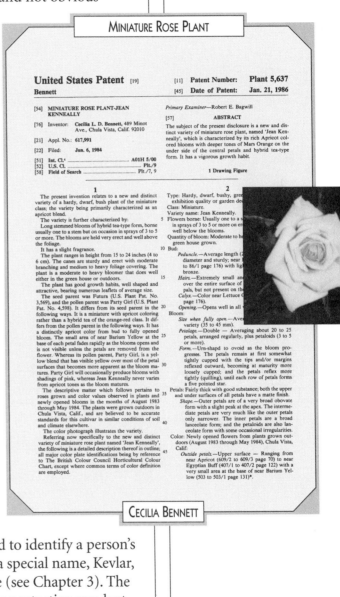

MINIATURE ROSE PLANT

CECILIA BENNETT

TRADEMARK/SERVICE MARK
APPLICATION, PRINCIPAL
REGISTER, WITH DECLARATION

MARK (Word(s) and/or Design)

CLASS NO.
(If known)

TO THE ASSISTANT SECRETARY AND COMMISSIONER OF PATENTS AND TRADEMARKS:

APPLICANT'S NAME:

APPLICANT'S BUSINESS ADDRESS:
(Display address exactly as
it should appear on registration)

APPLICANT'S ENTITY TYPE:   (Check one and supply requested information)

Individual - Citizen of (Country):

Partnership - State where organized (Country, if appropriate):
Names and Citizenship (Country) of General Partners:

Corporation - State (Country, if appropriate) of Incorporation:

Other (Specify Nature of Entity and Domicile):

GOODS AND/OR SERVICES:

Applicant requests registration of the trademark/service mark shown in the accompanying drawing in the United States Patent and
Trademark Office on the Principal Register established by the Act of July 5, 1946 (15 U.S.C. 1051 et. seq., as amended) for the
following goods/services (SPECIFIC GOODS AND/OR SERVICES MUST BE INSERTED HERE):

BASIS FOR APPLICATION:   (Check boxes which apply, but never both the first AND second boxes, and supply requested information
related to each box checked.)

[ ] Applicant is using the mark in commerce on or in connection with the above identified goods/services.  (15 U.S.C. 1051(a), as
amended.)  Three specimens showing the mark as used in commerce which the U.S. Congress may regulate (for example, interstate or between
the U.S. and a foreign country).
 •Date of first use of the mark in commerce:
 •Specify the type of commerce:
       (for example, interstate or between the U.S. and a specified foreign country)
 •Date of first use anywhere (the same as or before use in commerce date):
 •Specify manner or mode of use of mark on or in connection with the goods/services:
       (for example, trademark is applied to labels, service mark is used in advertisements)

[ ] Applicant has a bona fide intention to use the mark in commerce on or in connection with the above identified goods/services.
(15 U.S.C. 1051(b), as amended.)
 •Specify intended manner or mode of use of mark on or in connection with the goods/services:
       (for example, trademark will be applied to labels, service mark will be used in advertisements)

[ ] Applicant has a bona fide intention to use the mark in commerce on or in connection with the above identified goods/services,
and asserts a claim of priority based upon a foreign application in accordance with 15 U.S.C. 1126(d), as amended.
 • Country of foreign filing:                              • Date of foreign filing:

[ ] Applicant has a bona fide intention to use the mark in commerce on or in connection with the above identified goods/services
and, accompanying this application, submits a certification or certified copy of a foreign registration in accordance with 15
U.S.C. 1126(e), as amended.
 • Country of registration:                               • Registration number:

NOTE: Declaration, on Reverse Side, MUST be Signed

U.S. DEPARTMENT OF COMMERCE/Patent and Trademark Office

PTO Form 1478 (REV. 8/93)
OMB No. 0651-0009 (Exp. 6/30/95)

◆ Sample trademark application form.

Someone wanting to use a particular name as a trademark can check the files at the Patent and Trademark Office to make sure that the name has not been registered. A trademark does not prevent someone else from manufacturing and selling a product, but it does keep anyone else from using a product's name.

Sometimes a special illustration or typeface becomes part of the trademark. Constance Moore's Koolips is an example. This special design is called a logo.

*Koolips*

If an inventor does not want anyone to know how she or he made an invention, even if it means not having patent protection, the inventor might protect it as a trade secret under state (rather than federal) law. This protection is often used for a product that no one would be able to duplicate unless she or he knew the secret. One example is Bette Nesmith Graham's Liquid Paper.

In 1951, Graham was earning a living as a typist. She often made mistakes and rubbed many a hole in her paper trying to erase them. So she used a trick she had learned as an art student. Artists use gesso, a mixture of plaster and glue, to cover their mistakes. Graham worked with a chemist to create a similar product that would cover typing errors easily and dry quickly. She began the Mistake Out Company (later renamed) in 1956.

Graham started out mixing her formula in her kitchen with the help of her son, Michael. They poured the liquid into small bottles, sold it to her friends, and took it to offices and office supply stores. Finally, Graham sold her Liquid Paper Corporation to The Gillette Company for $47.5 million.

She did not apply for a patent for her formula. She never disclosed it to the public. Her formula was protected as a trade secret.

## PUTTING AN IDEA TO WORK

Once a patent is awarded, how can an inventor make it profitable? Corporate inventors do not have to worry about that. The corporation for which they work owns the patent and takes care of manufacturing and marketing the product. For individual inventors, this is much more of a problem. In fact, many inventors never profit from their inventions because they do not have the resources, patience, or time to go through the process of getting a patent and finding a manufacturer for the product. Often the best way to make a profit is to sell or license the idea or the patent to a manufacturing and marketing company.

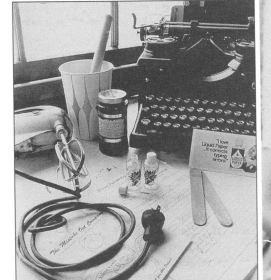

Licensing an idea to someone else (a company or an individual) gives the licensee certain rights in exchange for a reward, usually money. For example, you might license the rights to your patent to The Big Deal Company. The license gives the company permission to become the exclusive manufacturer and distributor of your product. In turn, the company agrees to pay you fifteen cents for each item sold. Or perhaps, instead of a per-item payment, you will receive twelve percent of the net profits. Ongoing payments for use of a license are called royalties.

Inventors often need special financial support to move from the idea stage to the testing, patent-

◆ Bette Nesmith Graham with her son, Michael, who helped her make and sell a liquid that could be painted on typing errors to hide them. Liquid Paper, as it was named, made Graham a millionaire. The formula does not have patent protection but is a trade secret.

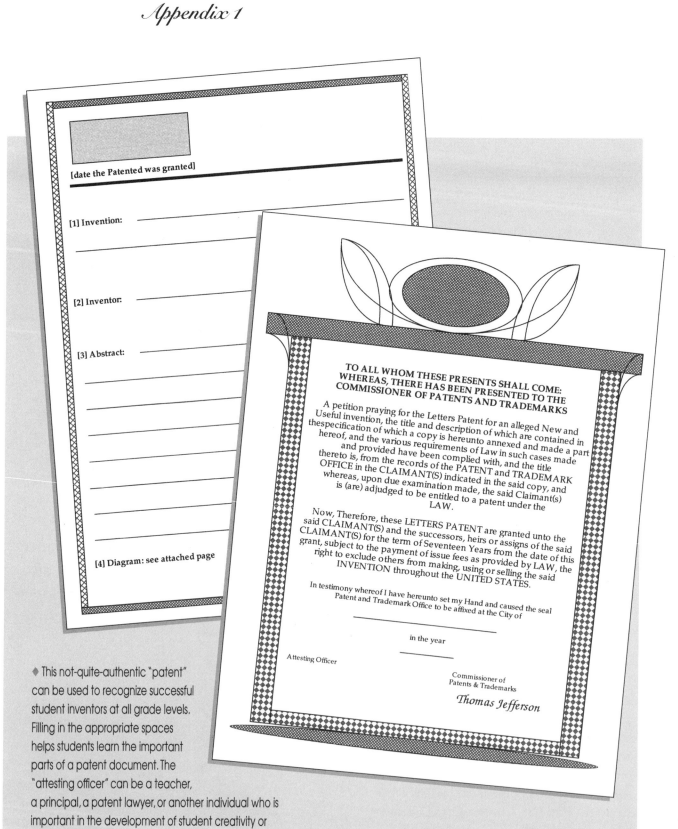

[date the Patented was granted]

[1] Invention:

[2] Inventor:

[3] Abstract:

[4] Diagram: see attached page

TO ALL WHOM THESE PRESENTS SHALL COME:
WHEREAS, THERE HAS BEEN PRESENTED TO THE
COMMISSIONER OF PATENTS AND TRADEMARKS

A petition praying for the Letters Patent for an alleged New and Useful invention, the title and description of which are contained in the specification of which a copy is hereunto annexed and made a part hereof, and the various requirements of Law in such cases made and provided have been complied with, and the title thereto is, from the records of the PATENT and TRADEMARK OFFICE in the CLAIMANT(S) indicated in the said copy, and whereas, upon due examination made, the said Claimant(s) is (are) adjudged to be entitled to a patent under the LAW.

Now, Therefore, these LETTERS PATENT are granted unto the said CLAIMANT(S) and the successors, heirs or assigns of the said CLAIMANT(S) for the term of Seventeen Years from the date of this grant, subject to the payment of issue fees as provided by LAW, the right to exclude others from making, using or selling the said INVENTION throughout the UNITED STATES.

In testimony whereof I have hereunto set my Hand and caused the seal Patent and Trademark Office to be affixed at the City of

_____

in the year

_____

Attesting Officer

Commissioner of
Patents & Trademarks

*Thomas Jefferson*

♦ This not-quite-authentic "patent" can be used to recognize successful student inventors at all grade levels. Filling in the appropriate spaces helps students learn the important parts of a patent document. The "attesting officer" can be a teacher, a principal, a patent lawyer, or another individual who is important in the development of student creativity or entrepreneurship.

ing, and marketing stages. A variety of agencies can provide help. Of special interest is the Research Corporation.

Frederick Gardner Cottrell was an inventor who wanted his work to benefit humanity. He helped make our air cleaner by inventing a way of controlling industrial air pollution — the Electrostatic Precipitator for Controlling Industrial Air Pollution. In 1912, he decided to use the profits from his invention to help other scientists do research that could help humanity. With the help of the Smithsonian Institution, he set up the Research Corporation to provide financial support for scientific research. Other scientists have contributed to this tax-exempt foundation.

Cottrell's goal in founding the Research Corporation was to promote the practical use of discoveries resulting from research, using patent royalties as a way of paying for other basic research. The Research Corporation makes several different kinds of awards. For example, through its Partners in Science Program, it awards money to college and university scientists to give qualified high school science teachers an opportunity to participate in research at a college or university during the summer.

Many inventors would not have been able to realize their inventions if not for the help of the Research Corporation. Rachel Brown and Elizabeth Hazen, inventors of a medicine to fight fungal infections (see Chapter 3), turned to the foundation for help in getting patent protection while they worked on the development of their drug.

The Research Corporation's support of Brown and Hazen made the foundation more conscious of the need to encourage the work of women inventors. Consequently, it was one of the major sponsors of an exhibition honoring women inventors at the 1990 Patent and Trademark Office's bicentennial celebration. The exhibition was titled "A Woman's Place Is in the Patent Office."

The Research Corporation's main office is at 101 N. Wilmot Road, Suite 250, Tucson, AZ 85711.

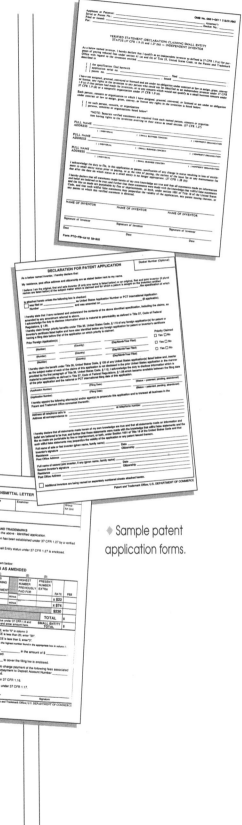

◆ Sample patent application forms.

# 2

# COULD YOU

ANYONE CAN BE AN INVENTOR — ANYONE with imagination, persistence, and a willingness to learn the needed technology. You can be an inventor if

☞ you are curious about how things work;

☞ you are not afraid to ask questions;

☞ you are not discouraged because everything you need to learn does not come easily;

☞ you read everything you can about subjects that interest you;

☞ you take advantage of opportunities for education and employment;

☞ you make opportunities for yourself if necessary.

To prepare yourself for what you want to be, you should

☞ try to meet people who are doing things you are interested in and make the most of personal contacts;

☞ take advantage of volunteer opportunities, such as working in a design studio, at a laboratory, in a hospital, or at an animal clinic;

☞ ask a librarian about guides to summer employment and to summer volunteer opportunities;

☞ go to school officials or teachers and say, "I'm really interested in working in (your area of interest)";

☞ form a club with science as a focus;

☞ seek out internships;

☞ go to museums and take part in their programs;

☞ take part in invention competitions (see pages 146–152).

# BE AN INVENTOR?

What makes science interesting is not what is known but what is not known. Inventors are the type of people for whom one question always leads to another. This often leads to the study of the basic laws of nature, or physics, and gaining knowledge in chemistry and all other areas of science and engineering. Math is an extremely important tool for people working in fields from new housing design to creative agriculture. You do not have to be a mathematical genius to work in the sciences, but you do need to become familiar with the language of mathematics.

## THE RISING SPIRIT

Inventing is in! Competitions are held throughout the country to encourage creative thinking and problem solving (see pages 146–152). Why? Because we live in a world of constant change. Every advancement in technology leads to new challenges. The problems facing the world are enormous. Our country's future depends on the development of new products and the improvement of old ones.

Young people with curious minds who like to tinker should take part in these programs. Besides being fun and challenging, they are a great way to make contact with people who can encourage and help you along as you continue your education and gain work experience.

Young women, working individually or in teams, have come up with some extremely interesting ideas during the past few years.

### The Cosmic Commode

In 1994, eighth-graders Nicole Leigh Orr, Kimberly Ellen Kolbeck, Kimberley Erin Brewer, and Megan Marie Gartner created excitement with their Cosmic Commode. From Patrick Henry Middle School in Sioux Falls, South Dakota, they were the first-place team for the middle grade level in the Second Annual ExploraVision Awards. This competition is sponsored by the Toshiba Corporation and the National Science Teachers Association (NSTA) "to develop in young people an interest in

> *The problems facing the world are enormous. Our country's future depends on the development of new products and the improvement of old ones.*

science and technology, the value of teamwork, and the ability to solve problems." There are categories for the primary, upper elementary, middle, and high school grade levels.

The girls' invention is described by the program's sponsors as "an ecologically sound, sanitary, user friendly toilet." It has its own wastewater treatment and recycling system. It comes equipped with a hand-held ultraviolet light scanner, which a person can use to kill bacteria on the toilet seat. With the touch of a button on the toilet, pregnancy, diabetes, and other urine-based tests can be performed and the results sent to a doctor. Also, the toilet is able to tell a person's weight. The Cosmic Commode is voice-activated and responds to commands such as "flush," "shut," and "weigh."

Seventh-grade girls from the Closter (New Jersey) Village School were regional winners in the contest. Their invention was "an umbrella that keeps you really dry, holds itself up, and won't flip inside out in the wind: The Super Umbrella! The umbrella of 2014 has a gutter along its rim that collects water and then drains it off via two gutter extensions. A zip-on, transparent, tinted, ultraviolet cover blocks both wind and sun. This sturdy umbrella can be attached to your shoulders with its tough plastic, snap-on, adjustable straps. Or, to avoid the extra weight, just use the attachable handle. The umbrella also folds up compactly for easy transporting." On the team were Amy C. Lenander, Shari Faye Ravner, Tana Xaka, and Kristen R. Accordino.

### Medical Imaging Technology: Pictures That Could Save Your Life

A group of girls from the Thomas Jefferson High School for Science and Technology in Alexandria, Virginia, were regional winners in the 1994 ExploraVision competition. The description of their product, "a sort of 'flight simulator' for future surgeons," says that "medical students can use this system to practice on three-dimensional computerized bodies that react to incisions just like a real patient would. Using virtual reality, doctors might conduct many procedures without ever having to come into physical contact with patients. Instead, doctors at surgical work stations elsewhere in the hospital could manipulate a special computerized joystick located at the operating site."

### Prosthetics: Rebuilding the Body

In 1993, tenth-grade girls from Warwick (Rhode Island) Veterans Memorial High School won first place in the high school category of the national ExploraVision Awards program. "Artificial limbs may not

be so artificial anymore," they proclaim in their invention description. Their invention would replace today's electrically powered prostheses (artificial limbs) with permanently attached, computer-controlled ones. Made of synthetic bone, cultured human skin, muscle fibers, and simulated joints, the limbs would look and feel like the real thing. The team consisted of Mary Ellen Morris, Lynn Marsella, Laurel Haley, and Emily Gallagher.

## MONEY TALKS

Another program that gives young people a chance to use their skills and knowledge is the Annual Duracell/NSTA Scholarship Competition. To enter, ninth- through twelfth-grade students must design and build a device that is educational, useful, or entertaining and is powered by one or more Duracell batteries. The prizes range from $100 savings bonds, given to fifty-nine students, to a $20,000 savings bond, given to the winner. The competition is designed to encourage young inventors and support students in developing hands-on science skills.

The 1994 winner was Tracy Phillips, from Long Beach (New York) High School. Her entry was Money Talks, an electronic device to help blind people handle money.

The device, neatly built into a wallet, tells the denomination (value) of each bill placed in the wallet. It works by using an infrared light emitter/detector, which lets varying amounts of light pass through the printed patterns of a bill, identifying key points that distinguish the bill's denomination. The amount of light passing through each point is measured by converting light energy to electrical energy. The signals are sent to a digital logic circuit, which matches codes and identifies the bill. The logic circuit activates a voice chip. The device is powered by four Duracell AAA batteries.

Tracy built the device because her younger brother is blind. "I have always wanted to do something for blind people, so I decided to combine that with my interest in electronics," she says. "In today's technological world, we have change machines giving us quarters for dollar bills to play video games. We even have talking computers that tell us the car door is ajar. Why can't we utilize these technologies to make an inexpensive, portable device to help blind people determine the denomination of paper money?"

Tracy plays the piano and belongs to the environmental and math clubs at school. She wants to be an engineer or a math teacher.

# INVENTION PROGRAMS AND CONTESTS

Following is a list of programs and contests that help create an enthusiasm for invention in young people. Take part in these programs. Find out just what you can do if you put your mind to it. You might be surprised!

## The B. F. Goodrich Collegiate Inventors Program

Paul Kunce
Inventure Place
221 S. Broadway
Akron, OH 44308
(216) 762-4463

## The Center for Studies in Creativity

Buffalo State College
1300 Elmwood Avenue
Chase Hall 244
Buffalo, NY 14222
(716) 878-6223

## Connecticut Invention Convention

c/o Phoenix Equity Planning Corp.
Michelle Munson, Chair
Mailstop 2E207
100 Bright Meadow Blvd.
Enfield, CT 06083
(203) 793-5299

## Duracell/NSTA Scholarship Competition

National Science Teachers Association
1840 Wilson Blvd.
Arlington, VA 22201
(703) 243-7100

## Franklin Institute Science Museum

222 N. 20th Street
Philadelphia, PA 19103-1194
(215) 448-1200

## FutureMakers: Inventor/Mentor Program

Gail Whitney, Project Director
Saturday Academy
Oregon Graduate Institute
P.O. Box 91000
Portland, OR 97291-1000
(503) 690-1190

## Future Scientists and Engineers of America

George Westrom, Executive Director
P.O. Box 9577
Anaheim, CA 92812
(714) 229-2223

## Gifted Youth Programs

Inventors Association of St. Louis
P.O. Box 16544
St. Louis, MO 63105
(314) 432-1291

## Invent, Iowa!

Dr. Nicholas Colangelo, Program Director
The Connie Belin Center
The University of Iowa
210 Lindquist Center
Iowa City, IA 52242-1529
(319) 335-6148
1-800-336-6463

## Inventing in the Biomedical Field

Jim Holte, Associate Professor
Department of Electrical Engineering
Electrical Engineering/Computer Science Building
200 Union Street, SE
Minneapolis, MN 55455
(612) 625-0811

## Inventor's Helpline

1-800-869-3900
(Calls from Virginia, Washington, D.C., and Maryland not accepted.)

## Inventors Clubs of America, Inc.

Dr. Alexander T. Marinaccio, Chairman and Founder
P.O. Box 450261
Atlanta, GA 31145-0261
(404) 938-5089

## Inventors Council of Dayton

140 E. Monument Avenue
Dayton, OH 45402
(513) 224-8513

## Inventors Workshop

International Education Foundation
7332 Mason Avenue
Canoga Park, CA 91306-2822

## Inventure Place

National Inventors Hall of Fame
Education Department
221 S. Broadway
Akron, OH 44308
(216) 762-4463

## Minnesota Academic Excellence Foundation

A Public Private Partnership
971 Capitol Square Building
550 Cedar Street
St. Paul, MN 55101
(612) 297-1875

## Minnesota Inventors Congress and Resource Center

P.O. Box 71
Redwood Falls, MN 56283-0071
1-800-468-3681

## Minnesota Student Inventors Congress

Kate Martens, State Coordinator
South Central ECSU
1610 Commerce Drive
North Mankato, MN    56003
(507) 389-1425

## National Inventive Thinking Association

Young Inventors' and Creators'
    Program
Leonard Molotsky, Executive
    Director
P.O. Box 836202
Richardson, TX 75083-836202

## National Society of Professional Engineers

Russel C. Jones, Deputy Executive
    Director
1420 King Street
Alexandria, VA 22314-2794

## New Hampshire Young Inventors' Program

Susan Zehnder, Director
Academy of Applied Science
98 Washington Street
Concord, NH 03301
(603) 225-2072

◆ Kirsten Albano, a participant in the
New Hampshire Young Inventors'
Program, displays her invention,
Safe-T-Trax.

## NUDGE Youth Program

William F. O'Keefe, Director
2211 O'Keefe Place
Zephyrhills, FL 33540
(813) 783-1731

## Orange County Invention Convention

Jim Nelson
Orange County Public Schools
445 W. Amelia Street
Orlando, FL 32801
(407) 849-3339

## Pennsylvania Inventors' Association

Charles Duryea
10819 Wales Road
Erie, PA 16510
(814) 739-2928

## Project XL

Ruth N. Nyblod
U.S. Patent and Trademark Office
Office of Public Affairs
Washington, DC 20231
(703) 305-8341

## San Diego Invention Program

San Diego Unified School District
Jo Anne Schaper, Elementary School Resource Teacher
Education Center, Room 2005
4100 Normal Street
San Diego, CA 92103-2682
(619) 264-0103

## The SBG Invention Convention

Silver Burdett & Ginn
Karen Schenk
299 Jefferson Road
Parsippany, NJ 07054
(201) 739-8192

## Student Inventions Through Education (SITE)

Educational Information Resource Center
Michael Waters
606 Delsea Drive
Sewell, NJ 08080
(609) 582-7000, ext. 130

## Toshiba NSTA ExploraVision Awards

National Science Teachers Association
1840 Wilson Blvd.
Arlington, VA 22201
(703) 243-7100

## Tualatin Invention Program

Tualatin Elementary School
Evelyn Andrews
19945 S.W. Boones Ferry Road
Tualatin, OR 97062
(503) 684-2359

## Venture Exchange Forum

Mike Howard, President
830 Corridor Park Blvd.
Knoxville, TN 37932
(615) 966-5429

### Western New York Invention Convention Program

Buffalo Public Schools
Marion Canedo, Early Childhood Director
428 City Hall
Buffalo, NY 14202
(716) 851-3626

### Young Inventors Program and Fair

Margaret Kuhfeld
Metro Educational Cooperative Service Unit (ECSU)
3499 Lexington Avenue North
St. Paul, MN 55126-8017
(612) 490-0058, ext. 107

### Youth Education Program

Inventors Association of New England
P.O. Box 335
Lexington, MA 02173
(617) 229-6614

The above listings are based on 1995 information and are subject to change.

*Appendix*

# 3 RESOURCES

## BOOKS

### Women in Science and Technology

Billings, Charlene W. *Grace Hopper: Navy Admiral and Computer Pioneer.* Hillside, New Jersey: Enslow Publishers, 1989.

Dash, Joan. *The Triumph of Discovery: Women Who Won the Nobel Prize.* Englewood Cliffs, New Jersey: Julian Messner, 1990.

Gallop, Nancy. *Science Is Women's Work: Photos and Biographies of American Women in the Sciences.* Windsor, California: National Women's History Project, 1994. Includes stories of outstanding scientists in astronomy, ecology, anthropology, mathematics, physics, chemistry, biology, and more. For information, contact the National Women's History Project, 7738 Bell Road, Windsor, CA 95492, (707) 838-6000.

Haber, Louis. *Women Pioneers of Science.* New York: Harcourt Brace Jovanovich, 1979.

Keller, Mollie. *Marie Curie.* New York: Franklin Watts, 1982. About the Polish-born chemist who was awarded the Nobel Prize in 1903 for the discovery of radium.

Macdonald, Anne L. *Feminine Ingenuity.* New York: Ballantine Books, 1992. A scholarly overview of women inventors in America in the context of social history, with many illustrations.

Moussa, Farag. *Women Inventors Honored by the World Intellectual Property Organization.* Geneva, Switzerland: Coopi, 1991. For information, contact the National Congress of Inventors Organizations (NCIO), 710 North 600 West, Logan, UT 84321.

Panabaker, Janet. *Inventing Women: Profiles of Women Inventors.* Ontario, Canada: Women Inventors Project, 1991.

Vance, Marguerite. *The Lamp Lighters: Women in the Hall of Fame.* New York: E.P. Dutton, 1960.

Vare, Ethlie Ann, and Greg Ptacek. *Women Inventors and Their Discoveries.* Minneapolis: The Oliver Press, 1993.

Veglahn, Nancy. *Women Scientists.* New York: Facts On File, 1991. About eleven women in science, from botany to solid-state physics, including Margaret Mead and Rosalyn Yalow.

### Women in the Fight for Equality

Archer, Jules. *Breaking Barriers: The Feminist Revolution From Susan B. Anthony to Margaret Sanger and Betty Friedan.* New York: Viking, 1991. About women who played major roles in the struggle for equality and for changes in the way women are viewed by society.

Ash, Maureen. *Story of the Women's Movement.* Chicago: Childrens Press, 1989. Traces the women's movement from its early history in the 1820s in England through the events of the twentieth century in the United States. Discussion of the Equal Rights Amendment. Valuable for curriculum reports and current events background.

Bloomer, D.C. *Life and Writings of Amelia Bloomer.* New York: Schocken Books, 1975. About an influential advocate of women's rights whose name is connected with a garment she advocated.

Bundles, A'Lelia Perry. *Madam C.J. Walker.* New York: Chelsea House, 1991. The story of Madam Walker's journey from poverty to fame and fortune as told by her great-great-granddaughter.

De Pauw, Linda Grant. *Founding Mothers.* Boston: Houghton Mifflin, 1975. Describes the life of Colonial and American Indian women during the Revolutionary era.

### Women and Technology in Space

Behrens, June. *Sally Ride, Astronaut: An American First.* Chicago: Childrens Press, 1984. An illustrated biography of the astrophysicist who, in June 1983, was the first woman and the youngest American astronaut to orbit the earth.

Briggs, Carole S. *At the Controls: Women in Aviation.* Minneapolis: Lerner Publications, 1991. About barnstorming, military pilots, test pilots, astronauts, airline captains, and aviation pioneers.

Fox, Mary Virginia. *Women Astronauts Aboard the Shuttle.* New York: Julian Messner, 1984; rev. 1988.

Pogue, William R. *How Do You Go to the Bathroom in Space?* New York: Tom Doherty Associates, 1985. Answers to many questions about living in space, based on the author's own experiences on space missions.

Ride, Sally. *To Space and Back: U.S. Astronaut Sally Ride Shares the*

*Adventures of Outer Space.* New York: Lothrup, Lee & Shepard, 1986. An account of a space journey, from blastoff to return to earth, aboard the space shuttle. Ride tells about things such as eating from a spoon floating in midair and putting on a space suit.

Schulke, Flip and Debra, and Penelope and Raymond McPhee. *Your Future in Space: The U.S. Space Camp Training Program.* New York: Crown Publishers, 1986. Girls especially will enjoy reading Kathryn Sullivan's account (in the foreword) of how she became an astronaut. This book tells about the U.S. Space Camp in Huntsville, Alabama, where children and adults learn to use equipment such as a space shuttle simulator.

Skurzynski, Gloria. *Zero Gravity.* New York: Bradbury Press, 1994. Describes what it is like to be in a zero-gravity environment as an astronaut orbiting earth in a space shuttle.

## Inventing and Related Subjects

Ardis, Susan B. *Inventive Women: American Female Patent Holders.* Englewood, Colorado: Teacher Ideas Press, 1995. An overview of women inventors in America, with personal details about their lives and a broad range of inventions.

Baker, Charles F. III, and Rosalie F. Baker. *Classical Ingenuity: The Legacy of Greek and Roman Architects, Artists, and Inventors.* Peterborough, New Hampshire: Cobblestone Publishing, 1993.

Bender, Lionel. *Invention.* New York: Alfred A. Knopf, 1991. A look at the way inventors have changed the world.

Burnie, David. *Light.* New York: Dorling Kindersley, 1992. Discusses reflecting light, splitting light, particle waves, diffraction and interference, electromagnetic waves, and holograms, among other topics.

Cassidy, John. *Explorabook: A Kids' Science Museum in a Book.* Palo Alto, California: Klutz Press, 1991. Includes activities in magnetism, light waves, illusions, biology, and more.

Clements, Gillian. *The Picture History of Great Inventors.* New York: Alfred A. Knopf, 1994. Illustrates and discusses great inventions from ancient times to the present.

Endacott, Geoff. *Discovery and Inventions.* New York: Viking, 1991. Includes many facts about inventions old and new, with illustrations.

*The Great Inventions.* London: Dorling Kindersley; distributed by Houghton Mifflin, Boston, 1993. Explains the origins of eight inventions and how they work.

*Grist Mills of Early America and Today.* Lebanon, Pennsylvania: Applied Arts Publishers, 1978. Includes a clear explanation of the technology, as well as recipes and illustrations of early mills.

*Historical Inventions on File Collection.* N.p.: The Diagram Group, 1994. Includes 125 line drawings, biographical information, a time line for each inventor, and a chronology of technology leading up to each invention. For information, call 1-800-443-8323; fax, 1-800-678-3633.

*Historical Science Experiments on File Collection.* N.p.: The Diagram Group, 1993. Experiments, demonstrations, and projects for the school and home. Materials included are copyright free for educational purposes. For information, call 1-800-443-8323; fax, 1-800-678-3633.

Howard, Robert A. *Water Power: How It Works.* Wilmington, Delaware: The Eleutherian Mills–Hagley Foundation, 1979. A simplified explanation of waterpower for young people. For information, contact The Eleutherian Mills–Hagley

Foundation, P.O. Box 3630, Wilmington, DE 19807.

James, Peter, and Nick Thorpe. *Ancient Inventions.* New York: Ballantine Books, 1994. Organized by theme with more than three hundred illustrations, this book covers inventions from thousands of years B.C. to the age of Columbus.

Lafferty, Peter. *Force and Motion.* New York: Dorling Kindersley, 1992. Explores the forces that set the world in motion and how they can be harnessed. Among the forces discussed are gravity, weight and mass, friction, spinning tops, and spiraling.

Macaulay, David. *The Way Things Work.* Boston: Houghton Mifflin, 1988. A visual guide to the world of machines.

Marzio, Peter C. *Rube Goldberg: His Life and Work.* New York: Harper & Row, 1973.

Platt, Richard. *Smithsonian Visual Timeline of Inventions.* New York: Dorling Kindersley, 1994. A family reference book with numerous illustrations ranging from the first prehistoric tools to satellites and superconductors.

Randolph, Sallie G., and Nancy O'Keefe Bolick. *Shaker Inventions.* New York: Walker & Company, 1990.

Smithsonian Institution. *Science Activity Book.* New York: Galison Books, 1987. Experiments for middle-grade students. Also, *More Science Activities,* 1988.

Taylor, Barbara. *Be an Inventor.* New York: Harcourt Brace Jovanovich, 1987. Illustrations from *The Weekly Reader* lead children through the process of inventing.

U.S. Patent and Trademark Office. *Basic Facts About Patents.* Washington, D.C.: U.S. Department of Commerce, n.d.

U.S. Patent and Trademark Office. *General Information Concerning Patents.* Washington, D.C.: U.S.

Department of Commerce, n.d.

VanCleave, Janice. *Astronomy for Every Kid: 101 Easy Experiments.* New York: John Wiley & Sons, 1991. Ideas, projects, and activities for schools and science fairs. Why do planets spin? How hot is the sun? What keeps the moon in orbit around the earth? These and other questions are answered.

VanCleave, Janice. *Chemistry for Every Kid: 101 Easy Experiments.* New York: John Wiley & Sons, 1989. Includes the meaning of phase changes; the structure of matter; the working of acids, gases, and solutions; and more.

VanCleave, Janice. *Physics for Every Kid: 101 Easy Experiments.* New York: John Wiley & Sons, 1991. Ideas, projects, and activities for schools, science fairs, and individuals. Learn how magnets work, what keeps airplanes in the air, and more.

Weiss, Harvey. *Machines and How They Work.* New York: Crowell, 1983. Includes the lever, the inclined plane, the screw, the wheel, the axle, the wedge, and the pulley and their use in more complex machines such as derricks, bulldozers, and metal lathes.

Williams, Brian and Brenda. *The Random House Book of 1001 Wonders of Science.* New York: Random House, 1990. Includes illustrated explanations of atoms, electricity, inventions, energy, motion, and more.

Williams, Trevor I. *The History of Invention: From Stone Axes to Silicon Chips.* New York: Facts On File, 1987. Traces improvements through history in the fields of agriculture, communication, architecture, and many other fields.

Zubrowski, Bernie. *Clocks: Building and Experimenting With Model Timepieces.* New York: Morrow Junior Books, 1988. A Boston Children's Museum activity book.

## MAGAZINES

*American Heritage of Invention & Technology.* Quarterly. Published by American Heritage, Forbes Building, 60 Fifth Avenue, New York, NY 10011.

*COBBLESTONE: The History Magazine for Young People.* Monthly, September through May. Published by Cobblestone Publishing, Inc., 7 School Street, Peterborough, NH 03458. Of special interest are these issues: "Women Inventors," June 1994; "African American Inventors," February 1992; "Thomas Edison," February 1980; "Meet Albert Einstein," October 1987; "Benjamin Franklin," September 1992; "The Wright Brothers and the Story of Aviation," December 1984; "The Shakers," April 1983. Write to the publisher for a catalog of back issues or call 1-800-821-0115.

*FACES: The Magazine About People.* Monthly, September through May. Published by Cobblestone Publishing, Inc., 7 School Street, Peterborough, NH 03458. Of special interest is the September 1994 issue, "Great Inventions of the World." Write to the publisher for a catalog of back issues or call 1-800-821-0115.

*Inventors' Digest.* Bimonthly. Published by United Inventors Association of the USA, JMH Publishing Co., 4850 Galley Road, Suite 209, Colorado Springs, CO 80915.

*ODYSSEY: Science That's Out of This World.* Monthly, September through May. Published by Cobblestone Publishing, Inc., 7 School Street, Peterborough, NH 03458. Of special interest are these issues: "Women in Astronomy," March 1994; "Careers," March 1992; "Frontiers in Flight," April 1994. Write to the publisher for a catalog of back issues or call 1-800-821-0115.

## FREE PUBLICATIONS FROM NASA

For a list of NASA National and Regional Teacher Resource Centers or a brochure giving an overview of educational materials available from NASA, contact the Educational Programs Office, Teacher Resource Laboratory, Goddard Space Flight Center, Code 130.3, Greenbelt, MD 20771, (301) 286-8570.

Examples of materials available: *Suited for Space Walking,* a teacher's guide with activities; *The Opportunity to Soar,* aerospace technology careers; *Astronaut Facts,* short biographies of former and current astronauts; posters, slides, videotapes, and audiotapes about the space program.

## PUBLICATIONS FROM THE U.S. PATENT AND TRADEMARK OFFICE

Copies of U.S. Patent and Trademark Office publications, the *Inventive Thinking Curriculum Project* (in English or Spanish), a summary of the nine-module course *Black Innovators in Technology: Inspiring a New Generation,* and the *Inventive Thinking Resource Directory* are available at no cost to educators from Project XL, an outreach program of the Patent and Trademark Office and an integral part of the U.S. Department of Commerce's Private Sector Initiative Program. Project XL is designed to encourage the development of inventive thinking and problem-solving skills among America's youth. For copies of these publications (limit ten copies per request), write to Project XL, Office of Public Affairs, U.S. Patent and Trademark Office, Washington, DC 20231. For other information, write to this address or call (703) 305-8341.

# RESOURCES FROM THE SMITHSONIAN INSTITUTION

*Life Story.* CD/ROM, an interactive learning environment using audiovisual. Explores the discovery of the structure of DNA by Jim Watson and Francis Crick. Includes interviews with Watson, Crick, and other scientists. Also includes hands-on experiments and questions and answers. Created by Apple Computer, Luca Arts Entertainment Company, and Adrian Malone Productions at the Smithsonian Institution. For information, contact Sunburst Communications, 101 Castleton Street, Pleasantville, NY 10570, 1-800-321-7511 or (914) 747-3310 (call collect); fax, (914) 747-5349.

*Science in American Life Education Materials for Schools.* Interdisciplinary materials created by Smithsonian educators and multimedia developers. Materials combine hands-on science activities with primary source analysis in lessons that span the curriculum — from science, history, and social studies to drama, visual arts, and creative writing. Includes five kits, special issues of *Art to Zoo* magazine, and a curriculum guide. Published by Tom Snyder Productions, Inc., 80 Coolidge Hill Road, Watertown, MA 02172, 1-800-342-0236.

*Smithsonian Resource Guide for Teachers.* For grades 5 through 12. Developed by the National Science Resources Center. For information, contact the Smithsonian Institution, National Academy of Sciences, Arts and Industries Building, Room 1201, Washington, DC 20560.

# VIDEOS

*Apollo 13: To the Edge and Back.* An exciting account of the *Apollo 13* mission, during which the spacecraft was out of touch with mission control for a time and the astronauts' safe return to earth was in jeopardy. Available from WGBH Educational Television, P.O. Box 2284, South Burlington, VT 05407, 1-800-255-9424.

*Be an Inventor.* The theme is creativity, with primary emphasis on the inventing process. Shows inventions by students. For grades 2–6. Teacher's guide included. Available from Harcourt Brace Trade Division, Order Fulfillment, 6277 Sea Harbor Drive, Orlando, FL 32887-4300.

*Discovering Women.* A six-part series about women scientists. Includes physicist Melissa Franklin, biochemist Lynda Jordan, molecular biologist Lydia Zilla-Kamaroff, computational neuroscientist Misha Mahowald, archaeologist Patty Jo Watson, and geophysicist Marcia McNutt. Available from Films for the Humanities and Sciences, P.O. Box 2053, Princeton, NJ 08543-2053, 1-800-257-5126.

*Invention Video Series.* This three-volume series looks at inventions that changed the world, including digital music, 3-D computer graphics, the first electric guitar, solar cars, and much more. Behind-the-scenes stories about major inventors add to the interest. Available from Pitsco, P.O. Box 1328, Pittsburg, KS 66762.

*Out of This World: The Apollo Moon Landing.* Available from the Holiday Video Library, Finley Holiday Film Corporation, P.O. Box 619, Whittier, CA 90608, 1-800-345-6707.

*A Woman's Place.* Pays tribute to noted women of the past and points out that a woman's place is everywhere. Narrated by Julie Harris. Available from Cally Curtis Company, 1111 N. Las Palmas, Hollywood, CA 90038.

*Woman's Place.* Examines the traditional role of women in American society and shows how that role is changing. Narrated by Bess Myerson. Available from the American Broadcasting Company, TV, 1330 Avenue of the Americas, New York, NY 10019.

*Women's Work: Engineering.* Documentary designed to encourage young women to pursue a career in engineering. The video documents the personal and professional lives of several engineering students and working engineers. Available from the Massachusetts Institute of Technology Center for Advanced Engineering Study, 77 Massachusetts Avenue, Room 9-234, Cambridge, MA 02139, (617) 253-7444.

# CD-ROM

*It's Her Heritage: A Biographical Encyclopedia of Famous American Women.* Includes women in the arts, politics, sports, space, and science, from pioneer days to the present. With illustrations and film and newsreel footage. Available from Pilgrim New Media, 955 Massachusetts Avenue, Cambridge, MA 02139.

*See also* Resources From the Smithsonian Institution, this page.

# KITS

*The Boston Museum of Science: Inventor's Workshop.* Comes with an electric motor, gears, a propeller, and other materials to allow students to create useful devices by using their imagination. Available from Running Press, 125 S. Twenty-second Street, Philadelphia, PA 19103, 1-800-345-5359.

*OOZ & OZ Educational Kit.* Allows students to create their own anamorphic art (see Chapter 5). The technique is based on a classical concept. The image originates as a distortion, but when it is viewed in a specially shaped mirror, the reflection is not distorted. Provided in the kit are information on the history of the technology, instructions, a master grid for making a picture, a completed drawing as an example, and a packet of thirty Mylar (clear plastic) strips for reflecting the picture. For information, call 1-800-800-4199 or (201) 669-1198; fax, (201) 669-1290.

## PLACES TO VISIT

More than one hundred science and technology museums and centers are located across the country. Only a few are mentioned here. Check a museum guide for other places to visit.

*American Bicycle and Cycling Museum,* Santa Fe, New Mexico

*Ann Arbor Hands-on Museum,* Ann Arbor, Michigan

*Children's Science Center,* Cape Coral, Florida

*Comer Museum,* Morgantown, West Virginia

*Corning Glass Center,* Corning, New York

*Discovery Center of Science and Technology,* Syracuse, New York

*Exploration Station: A Children's Museum,* Bradley, Illinois

*Historical Electronics Museum,* Linthicum, Maryland

*Imaginarium,* Anchorage, Alaska

*Inventure Place: National Inventors Hall of Fame,* Akron, Ohio

*Junior Museum,* Troy, New York

*Museum of American Textile History,* North Andover, Massachusetts

*Museum of Early Trades and Crafts,* Madison, New Jersey

*National Museum of American History,* Smithsonian Institution, Washington, D.C.

*Pacific Science Center,* Seattle, Washington

*Science and Technology Museum of Atlanta,* Atlanta, Georgia

*Southwest Museum of Science and Technology, The Science Place,* Dallas, Texas

Of particular interest are museums taking part in the Seek Out Science (SOS) Museum Projects, which have been set up in connection with the *Discovering Women* TV series produced by WGBH in Boston. Exhibits at the following museums feature student science projects.

*California Museum of Science and Industry,* Los Angeles, California

*Chicago Academy of Sciences,* Chicago, Illinois

*The Children's Museum,* Boston, Massachusetts

*Children's Museum of San Diego,* San Diego, California

*Louisiana Arts & Science Center,* Baton Rouge, Louisiana

*The Oregon Museum of Science and Industry,* Portland, Oregon

*The Orlando Science Center,* Orlando, Florida

*The Witte Science Museum,* San Antonio, Texas

For more information, contact WGBH TV, Educational Print and Outreach Division, 125 Western Avenue, Boston, MA 02134.

## CAMPS

*Camp Ingenuity* is a weeklong science creativity and invention program for grades 7 through 9. *Camp Invention* is for grades 1 through 6. For information, contact the National Inventors Hall of Fame, 221 S. Broadway, Akron, OH 44308, (216) 762-4463.

## NATIONAL AND INTERNATIONAL INVENTORS ORGANIZATIONS

American Association of Inventors
2853 State Street
Saginaw, MI 48602
(517) 791-3444

Assists with the development of ideas, the patent application process, production, and marketing.

Inventors Clubs of America, Inc.
P.O. Box 450261
Atlanta, GA 30345
(404) 938-5089

Sponsors local clubs; conducts educational programs and competitions; maintains a library, biographical archive, and museum.

World Intellectual Property Organization
34, chemin des Colombettes
CH-1211 Geneva 20, Switzerland
22 7309 111

This specialized agency of the United Nations, with 116 members, is concerned with patents, trademarks, and copyrights. It administers treaties and offers technical assistance and training for member nations.

# Bibliography

Albertine, Susan. "An Unusually Inventive Mind: Harriet Williams Russell Strong." Unpublished manuscript, 1988.

Amram, Fred M.B. "Fantasizing Toward Power: Women Inventors Making a Difference." In *Bicentennial Proceedings, Events, and Addresses,* commemorative edition. Washington, D.C.: Port City Press, 1991.

Amram, Fred M.B. "Fostering Innovation in Technical Organizations: A North American Perspective." *Mindscope* (Malaysian Invention and Design Society), no. 15, July-September 1991.

Amram, Fred M.B. "From Household to High Tech: An Interdisciplinary Approach to Invention." *Mindscope* (Malaysian Invention and Design Society), no. 16, October-December 1991.

Amram, Fred M.B. "From Ironing to Transplants." *Mindscope* (Malaysian Invention and Design Society), no. 17, January-March 1992.

Amram, Fred M.B. "Invention as Problem-Solving: Special Contributions of Female Inventors." *Bulletin of Science, Technology, and Society,* vol. 7, 1988.

Amram, Fred M.B. "Technology and Values Visit the Patent and Trademark Office Bicentennial." In *Proceedings of the Fifth National Technological Literacy Conference,* 1990.

Billings, Charlene W. *Grace Hopper: Navy Admiral and Computer Pioneer.* Hillside, New Jersey: Enslow Publishers, 1989.

Bundles, A'Lelia Perry. *Madam C.J. Walker.* New York: Chelsea House, 1991.

De Pauw, Linda Grant. *Founding Mothers: Women of America in the Revolutionary Era.* Boston: Houghton Mifflin, 1975.

Gilbert, Lynn, and Gayler Moore. *Particular Passion: Talks With Women Who Have Shaped Our Times.* New York: Clarkson N. Potter, 1981.

Glazier, Stephen. *Random House Word Menu.* New York: Random House, 1992.

*Guide to Northern Liberties.* Philadelphia: Northern Liberties Neighbors Association, 1982.

Harte, Susan. "Patterned for Perfection." *Atlanta Journal, The Atlanta Constitution,* August 4, 1985.

Hindle, Brooke, ed. *America's Wooden Age: Aspects of Its Early Technology.* Tarrytown, New York: Sleepy Hollow Restoration, 1975.

"Knecht Steps Forward." *Women's Wear Daily,* July 29, 1991.

"Looking Back: G.M. Hopper's Young Years." *Chips: Magazine of Naval Computer and Command Telecommunication,* April 1992.

Macdonald, Anne L. *Feminine Ingenuity.* New York: Ballantine Books, 1992.

Moussa, Farag. *Women Inventors Honored by the World Intellectual Property Organization.* Geneva, Switzerland: Coopi, 1991.

"Navy Computer Pioneer, Innovator, Hopper Dies." *Sea Services Weekly,* January 17, 1992.

Needles, Samuel H. "The Governor's Mill and the Globe Mills, Philadelphia." *Pennsylvania Magazine of History and Biography,* October 1884.

Panabaker, Janet. *Inventing Women: Profiles of Women Inventors.* Ontario, Canada: Women Inventors Project, 1991.

Peacock, Mary. "Gabrielle Knecht's Patented Patterns." *Ms.,* March 1985.

"People." *Apparel Industry Magazine,* December 1987.

"Push Button Scrubbing: Inventor Building 'Self-Cleaning' House." *Los Angeles Times,* Section 1, November 1, 1981.

Randolph, Sallie G., and Nancy O'Keefe Bolick. *Shaker Inventions.* New York: Walker & Company, 1990.

Rothe, Anna, and Evelyn Lohr, eds. *Current Biography: Who's News and Why.* New York: H.W. Wilson Co., 1952.

Stanley, Autumn. *Mothers and Daughters of Invention: Notes for a Revised History of Technology.* Metuchen, New Jersey: Scarecrow Press, 1993.

Stern, Madeleine B. *We, the Women: Career Firsts of Nineteenth Century America.* New York: Schulte Publishing, 1963.

Tolles, Frederick B. "Sybilla Masters." In *Notable American Women, 1607–1950,* edited by Edward T. James. Cambridge, Massachusetts: The Belknap Press, Harvard University Press, 1971.

U.S. Patent and Trademark Office. *Buttons to Biotech: U.S. Patenting by Women, 1977 to 1988.* Washington, D.C.: U.S. Department of Commerce, 1990.

Van Horne, Gladys. "Maestra's New Suit Stitched Just in Time." *Wheeling News-Register,* September 23, 1992.

Whittaker, Walton. "Remarks made by Grace M. Hopper at the 'Seminar for Navy Computer Bosses.'" *Sea Services Weekly,* June 23, 1989.

## Answers to Chapter 1

**Puzzle 1: Can You Solve the Riddles?**
1. An idea.
2. When someone else invents a new device based on the person's invention. When this happens, the new invention and inventor are the only ones people hear about, even though the earlier invention made the newer one possible.
3. Anna Corey Baldwin, who invented four things having to do with milk: a way to make an ointment or a hair-slicking product; a way to make a cordial or a vinegar using milk whey; a milk cooler; a mechanical cow milker.

**Puzzle 2: Now What Did They Mean by That?**
1. "Show me your metal." Grooves or channels were cut into millstones to let air pass and carry off heat generated by friction during grinding. The ground flour or meal also escaped through these channels. The grooves or channels had to be sharpened. Men who cut the grooves and sharpened them were called "stone dressers." When they used a metal hammer to sharpen the stones, pieces of the hammer would sometimes chip off and get embedded in the stone dresser's hand. If a stone dresser asked a miller for work, claiming he was experienced in his trade, the miller would ask to see the man's hand, saying, "Show me your metal."
2. "Keep your nose to the grindstone." If the millstones were touching, heat would be generated by friction. The flour could easily catch fire from sparks. The miller had to smell the stones to detect heat — that is, literally "keep her or his nose to the grindstone."

**Puzzle 3: The Right Words**
1. Education, work experience, legal rights, and tradition are all correct.
2. Dyed, flattened, cut, split, braided, bleached, and boiled are all correct.
3. Modest.
4. Clothing.

## Answers to Chapter 2

**Puzzle 1: Unscramble Margaret Knight**
1. cotton mill
2. looms
3. square-bottomed
4. photography
5. knowledge
6. combustion

**Puzzle 2: Match the Problem With the Solution**

| | |
|---|---|
| 1. f | 5. c |
| 2. h | 6. b |
| 3. d | 7. a |
| 4. g | 8. e |

## Answers to Chapter 3

**Puzzle 1: Who *Was* That Woman?**
**Across**
2. hunch
5. repel soil
7. Patsy
10. gene
12. research teams
15. iron
17. Kwolek
18. Yamamoto
**Down**
1. chemist
3. persistence
4. Elion
6. fatty emulsion
7. polymers
8. Benerito
9. Hoover
11. language
13. software
14. Amazing
16. COBOL

**Puzzle 2: Relating the General to the Specific**

| | |
|---|---|
| 1. b | 3. d |
| 2. c | 4. a |

**Imagine That!: Make Yogurt**
You need a hot plate, a sink, balances, thermometers, a 3-quart pot, spoons, and an incubator or other way of keeping the yogurt at a constant temperature for a period of several hours. You could use electric heating pads over and under a lidded box, such as a photocopier-paper box. You will need to experiment to find the heating pad settings that will maintain a temperature of 99°F to 104°F for the time needed to convert milk to yogurt. Rombauer and Becker suggest using an insulated cooler.

## Answers to Chapter 4

**Puzzle 1: Guess Who**
1. Barbara Askins
2. Hatice Cullingford
3. Margaret Grimaldi
4. Jane Malin
5. Jeanne Crews
6. Eve Abrams Wooldridge
7. Karen Castell

**Puzzle 2: The Right Word**
**Across**
3. Crews
4. solar
6. Askins
9. autoradiograph
11. Eve Abrams
13. engineers
15. Karen

16. ozone
17. theory
**Down**
1. aeronautics
2. layers
5. voltage
7. Jane Malin
8. problems
10. pressure
12. memory alloy
13. escape pole
14. Grimaldi

**Puzzle 3: Match the Problem With the Solution**

| | |
|---|---|
| 1. d | 4. b |
| 2. e | 5. c |
| 3. a | |

## Answers to Chapter 5

**Puzzle 1: Word Scramble**

| | |
|---|---|
| 1. Togo | 3. plastic |
| 2. fascinated | 4. sleeve |

**Puzzle 2: Questions and Answers**

| | |
|---|---|
| 1. d | 4. a |
| 2. c | 5. e |
| 3. b | 6. f |

**Puzzle 3: An Anamorpho *What*?**
**Across**
1. ratio
4. existing
7. bonding
8. kit
10. Horn
11. Disclosure
12. anamorphoscope
15. Rozier
18. safety needle
19. Togo
20. play
23. sleeves
24. Knecht
**Down**
2. thermoforming
3. apnea
5. Snugli
6. Jagger
9. I.V. House
13. Moore
14. Hoffman
16. prototype
17. utility
21. Lisa
22. Pete